Title Index for the
Directory of Unpublished
Experimental Mental
Measures

Volumes 1–7

Martin Jamison
Ohio State University Libraries

Association of College
A division of the Ameri(
Chicagc

The paper used in this publication meets the minimum requirements of American National Standard for Information Sciences–Permanence of Paper for Printed Library Materials, ANSI Z39.48—1992.∞

Library of Congress Cataloging-in-Publication Data

Jamison, Martin.
  Title index for the Directory of unpublished experimental mental measures : volumes 1-7 / Martin Jamison.
    p. cm.
Includes index.
  ISBN 0-8389-8174-7 (alk. paper)
  1. Intelligence tests--indexes. 2. Psychological tests--Indexes. 3. Personality tests--Indexes. I. Directory of unpublished experimental mental measures. II. Title.
  BF431 .J29 2001
  016.15'028'7--dc21

                                                2001007290

Printed in the United States of America.

05 04 03 02 01   5 4 3 2 1

Preface

This is a cumulative title index to volumes one through seven of the *Directory of Unpublished Experimental Mental Measures*. Its purpose is to enable access, by title and entry number, to the testing instruments cited in the *Directory* volumes.

Since 1974 the *Directory of Unpublished Experimental Mental Measures* has provided useful information on noncommercial experimental scales. Although it offers excellent author and subject indexes to the test entries, it has no built-in index by test title.

Users of this index should be aware of certain characteristics:

• Wherever possible the compiler has resolved extremely slight variations of titles which prove to refer to the same scale. Where title variations are more complex, cross-references have been provided. Where reference to one and the same title could not be established, variant titles have been allowed to stand.

• Where variant titles have been allowed to stand, plurals and differences in spelling can cause similar-sounding entries to file in separate locations. For example, the plural form of some of the words cause an *Attitude toward Christianity Scale* to appear in four different alphabetical places.

• Titles beginning with a qualifier, such as "revised" or "modified," have been inverted except when an independent source indicates that the title actually does begin with the qualifier (for example, *Revised Self-Monitoring Scale*).

• References to particular subscales or forms have been entered under the names of the parent tests (for example, *Child Abuse Potential Inventory, Inconsistency Scale*).

• Numbers within test titles file in alphabetical order as though they were spelled out.

This index supplements the *Directory*'s subject and author indexes, but does not replace them. When searching for a scale by topic or when desiring more titles like one found in the title index, users should employ the *Directory*'s cumulative subject index.

The compiler is grateful for the release time provided by the Ohio State University Libraries for pursuit of this project. He also acknowledges the extensive collection of research journals housed in OSU's Education, Human Ecology, Psychology, and Social Work Library, which enabled title variations and other anomalies to be investigated.

Martin Jamison
Columbus, Ohio

A

A-B Rating Scale, 3450, 5164, 5165
AB Scale, 306
Abbreviated Temperament Questionnaire, 3342
Ability Self-Rating Inventory, 305
Ability to Cope Scale, 5445
Abortion Attitude Scale, 4229
Absence Attitude Scale, 4230
Absence Consequences Scale, 4118
Absorption Scale, 4745 [See also Tellegen Absorption Scale]
Abstract Orientation Scale, 2200
Abstract Reasoning Test, 884, 2201, 2202
Abuse and Use of Drugs Survey, 6187
Abusive Violence Scale, 4344
Academic Achievement Accountability Questionnaire, 467
Academic Achievement Accountability Scale, 1367
Academic Achievement Scale, 1337
Academic Adjustment Scale, 4231
Academic Advising Inventory, 6531
Academic and Social Integration Instrument, 2399
Academic and Social Integration Inventory, 4633
Academic Assistant Evaluation Instrument, 992
Academic Attitudes Scale, 6060
Academic Attribution Scale, 5399
Academic Autonomy Scale, 5400
Academic Barriers Questionnaire, 5894
Academic Curiosity Scale, 1984
Academic Interaction Inventory, 5166
Academic Internal-External (I-E) Control Scale, 1368

Academic Misconduct Survey, 6188, 6189
Academic Motivation Inventory, 1985
Academic Motivation Profile, 6532
Academic Motivation Scale, 3123, 6624
Academic Practices Survey, 6190
Academic Pressure Scale for Adolescents, 5446
Academic Procrastination Scale, 5401, 5402
Academic Self-Concept Scale, 2030, 3153, 4746, 6679, 6680
Academic Self-Description Questionnaires, 4747
Academic Self-Efficacy Scale, 4748, 6681, 6682
Academic Self-Esteem Scale, 2031, 3154, 4749
Academic Self-Image Test, 4750
Academic Self-Regulation Questionnaire, 4345
Academic Self-Schema, 3155
Academic Setting Evaluation Questionnaire, 6533
Academic Situational Constraints Scale, 6534
Academic Stress Scale, 3691
Academic Vocational Involvement Scale, 1574
Acceptability to Others Scale, 5702
Acceptance/Involvement Scale, 6385
Acceptance of Blame Measure, 907
Acceptance of Disability Scale, 1636
Acceptance of Illness Scale, 2432
Acceptance of Individual Differences Measure, 3963
Acceptance of Interpersonal Violence Scale, 3964, 6061
Acceptance of Marital Termination Scale, 2963
Acceptance Rating Scale, 3965

Accepting the Past and Reminiscing about the Past Scales, 6683
Accident Locus of Control Scale, 6684
Acculturation Attitudes Scale, 5703
Acculturation Measure, 1696
Acculturation Rating Scale for Mexican-Americans, 2547, 3966, 5704
Acculturation Rating Scale for Puerto Ricans, 3967
Acculturation Scale for Mexican-American Children, 3519
Acculturative Stress Scale, 5705
Achenbach Child Behavior Checklist, 2799 [See also Child Behavior Checklist, Ages 2–3]
Achievability of Future Goals Scale, 3156, 6625
Achievement Anxiety Test, 908, 1625, 2240, 3692–3694 [See also Alpert-Haber Achievement Anxiety Test]
Achievement Anxiety Test Scale—Revised, 2433
Achievement Attribution Scale, 3157
Achievement Goal Tendencies Questionnaire, 6626
Achievement Motivation Measure, 1338
Achievement Motivation Questionnaire, 1986, 4693
Achievement Motivation Scale, 1987, 3124, 3125, 4694, 6627 [See also Myers Achievement Motivation Scale]
Achievement Motivation Scale for Men—Revised, 1988
Achievement Motivation Scales, 4695
Achievement Motivation Test, 1989, 1990, 4696
Achievement Motive Questionnaire, 712
Achievement Motives Scale, 4697, 6628

Achievement-Orientation Questionnaire, 713
Achievement Orientation—Revised, 3126
Achieving Tendency Scales for Males and Females, 6629 [See also Mehrabian Achieving-Tendency Scale]
Acquaintance Description Form, 2548
Acquiescent Test, 278
ACT Unisex Interest Inventory, 3343
Action Control Scale, 4698
Activation-Deactivation Adjective Checklist, 1839, 2434
Activation-Deactivation Adjective Checklist, Short Form, 5447
Active Engagement Scale, 7117
Activities Index, 1339
Activities of Daily Living Scale, 3751
Activity and Drug Use Checklists, 6191
Activity-Feeling State Scale, 6630
Activity Level Questionnaire, 1203
Activity Preference Questionnaire, 6983
Activity Preference Scale, 3388
Activity Reaction Inventory, 1293
Activity Scale, 6192
Activity-Stereotypes Scale, 2032
Actual-Ideal Self Semantic Differential, 748
Adaptability to Change Questionnaire, 5448
Adaptation-Innovation Inventory, 7118 [See also Kirton Adaption-Innovation Inventory]
Adapted Shame and Guilt Scale, 5022
Adaptive Behavior Inventory for Children—Peer Group Role and Student Role Scales, 2590
Adaptive Regression Scale, 606
Adaptive Social Behavior Inventory, 5707, 6193

Adelaide-Conners Parent Rating Scale, 4346

Adjective Check List, 211

Adjective Check List for Campus Help Givers, 993

Adjective Check List, Intraception Scale, 3135

Adjective Checklist, 5449, 6984

Adjective Generation Technique, 1369

Adjective Rating Scale, 3049

Adjective Rating Scale for Self-Description, 749

Adjective Ratings Form, 5023

Adjustment Inventory, 5708

Adjustment Rating Scale, 403

Adjustment Scale, 3752

Adjustment Semantic Differential, 1067

Adjustment to College Life Measure, 3695, 5403

Adjustment to College Scale, 2400, 2401, 3696

Administrative Stress Index, 2617

Administrator Image Questionnaire, 1307

Adolescent Abuse Inventory, 2964

Adolescent Activities Checklist, 4347

Adolescent AIDS Survey, 5364

Adolescent Alienation Scale, 2549

Adolescent Behavioral Problems Scale, 6194

Adolescent Communication Inventory, 2897

Adolescent-Coping Orientation for Problem Experiences Scale, 6386

Adolescent Drug Use Questionnaire, 562

Adolescent Ego Identity Scale, 2241, 6985

Adolescent Egocentrism Scale, 5167

Adolescent Family Life Satisfaction Index, 6387

Adolescent Goal Attainment Scale, 2898

Adolescent Interpersonal Competence Questionnaire, 3968

Adolescent-Parent Interaction Questionnaire, 640

Adolescent-Parent Relations Scale, 6388

Adolescent Perceived Events Scale, 3753, 3754, 5450

Adolescent Perceived Stress Scale, 2435

Adolescent Risk Behavior and Attitudes Questionnaire, 6195

Adolescent Self-Perception Inventory, 5080

Adolescent Structure Inventory, 2175 [See also Chabassol Adolescent Structure Inventory]

Adorno F Scale, 909 [See also F-Scale]

Adult Attachment Scale, 5709

Adult-Attitudes toward Computers Survey, 6062

Adult Development Scale, 2943

Adult Inventory of Procrastination, 6196

Adult Irrational Ideas Inventory, 1637

Adult Nowicki-Strickland I-E Scale, 2033 [See also Nowicki-Strickland Internal-External...for Adults; Nowicki-Strickland Locus of Control Scale for Adults]

Adult Nowicki-Strickland Internal-External Control Scale—Abbreviated, 4751 [See also Nowicki-Strickland Internal-External...for Adults; Nowicki-Strickland Locus of Control Scale for Adults]

Adult Nowicki-Strickland Internal-External Locus of Control, 4752 [See also Nowicki-Strickland Internal-External...for Adults; Nowicki-Strickland Locus of Control Scale for Adults]

Adult Nowicki-Strickland Internal-External Scale, 6685 [See also Nowicki-Strickland Internal-External...for Adults; Nowicki-Strickland Locus of Control Scale for Adults]

Adult Orientation to Child Autonomy Scale, 2550

Adult Playfulness Scale, 6197

Adult Rating Scale, 6986

Adult Self-Expression Scale, 2242, 3451

Adult Self-Perception Profile, 6686

Adult Sources of Self-Esteem Inventory, 6687

Adult Survey of Reading Attitudes—Revised, 4232

Adult Version of the Nowicki-Strickland Internal-External Locus of Control Scale, 6693 [See also Nowicki-Strickland Internal-External...for Adults; Nowicki-Strickland Locus of Control Scale for Adults]

Adult Vocational Maturity Assessment Interview, 2618, 2944

Adult Vocational Maturity Inventory, 1936

Adversarial Sexual Beliefs and Acceptance of Rape Myths Scale, 6063

Adversarial Sexual Beliefs Scale, 4753

Adversarial Sexual Beliefs Scales, 6064

Advising Satisfaction Questionnaire, 1959

Advising Satisfaction Scale, 994

Advisor, 1572

Advisor Effectiveness Evaluation, 2329

Aesthetic Sensitivity Scale, 2034

Affect Adjective Checklist, 5451

Affect Balance Scale, 2436, 3755, 3756, 5452

Affect-Cognition Scale, 404

Affect Intensity Measure, 3757, 5024

Affect Intensity Measures, 5453

Affect Questionnaire, 6987

Affective and Continuance Commitment Scale, 7350 [See also Continuance Commitment Scale]

Affective Commitment Scale, 3609, 5305, 5454, 7351

Affective Commitment Scale—Revised, 5455

Affective Contents of Communication Scale, 4478

Affective Disposition Scale, 5456

Affective Entry Questionnaire, 3158

Affective Intimacy Index, 2965

Affective Organizational Commitment Scale, 7352

Affective Scale, 7353

Affective Self-Disclosure Scale for Couples, 6335

Affective Sensitivity Measure, 428

Affective Sensitivity Scale, 2243

Affective Sensitivity Scale, Adaptation of, 98

Affective Sensitivity Scale, Form C, 429

Affective States Inventory, 1638

Affective Work Competencies Inventory, 3520

Affiliation Scale, 5710

Affiliative Tendency Scale, 44, 1697

Affinity-Seeking Scale, 6631

AFI-65 Scale, 641

African Self-Consciousness Scale, 4754, 6688

After-College Questionnaire, 4755

Age of Initial Drug Use Questionnaire, 1204

Agency Climate Questionnaire, 3050

Aggression-Anxiety Scale, 2437

Aggression Assessment Scale, 1840

Aggression Inventory, 7149

Aggression, Moodiness, Learning Problems Scale (AML), 2801

Aggression-Potential Measure, 1476
Aggression Word Association Test, 3452
Aggressive Act Report, 2800
Aggressive Behavior Scale, 3453
Aggressive Orientation Scale, 7150
Aggressive Sexual Behavior Inventory, 4348
Agitation Behavior Mapping Instrument, 4349
Agoraphobic Cognitions Questionnaire, 2438, 3758
Agoraphobic Cognitions Scale, 6988
Agreement/Disagreement Test, 483
Agreement Response Scale, 2244 [See also Couch-Kiniston Agreement-Response Test]
Agreement Response Scale—Revised, 3344
AID Measure, 995
AIDS and Homosexuality Attitude Scale, 4233
AIDS Attitudes and Conservative Views Scale, 6065
AIDS Attitudes and Knowledge Scale, 6066
AIDS Attribution Scale, 6689
AIDS Knowledge Questionnaire, 5366
AIDS Knowledge Test, 5365
AIDS Prevention Survey, 5367
AIDS Psychosocial Scale, 5711
AIDS Risk Knowledge Test, 5368
AIDS Victim Employment Scale, 4756
Alcadd Test, 1639
Alcohol and Drug Use Questionnaire, 563
Alcohol, Cigarettes, and Coffee Attitude Scales, 1122
Alcohol Expectancies for Social Evaluative Situations, 6690
Alcohol Expectancy Questionnaire, 3159, 6691
Alcohol Expectancy Questionnaire for Adolescents, 3160

Alcohol Expectancy Questionnaire—Revised, 6692
Alcoholism Treatment Survey, 4350
Alienation and Drug Use Questionnaire, 1698
Alienation and Self-Estrangement Questionnaire, 430
Alienation Scale, 45, 1090, 1699, 3969, 5712 [See also Dean's Alienation Scale; Scale of Alienation]
Alienation Scales, 1700, 1701
Alienation Test, 5713
Alpert-Haber Achievement Anxiety Test, 387, 2439 [See also Achievement Anxiety Test]
Alpert-Haber Achievement Anxiety Test, Debilitating Anxiety Scale of, 1626
Altruism Scale, 6989
Alzheimer's Disease Survey, 3666
Ambiguity Tolerance Scale, 2245, 7151–7153 [See also AT-20; Intolerance of Ambiguity…; Revised Scale for Ambiguity Tolerance; Scale of Tolerance-Intolerance of Ambiguity; Tolerance for Ambiguity …]
Ambivalence over Emotional Expressiveness Questionnaire, 6990
American-International Relations Scale, 5714
American University of Beirut Trial Aptitude Battery, 1732
Ames Philosophical Belief Inventory, 968, 2296
Amount of Information Obtained Scale, 7354
Amount of Invested Mental Effort Scale, 3161
Amsterdam Child Behavior Checklist, 6198
Anagram Fluency Test, 1903
Analogical Reasoning Test, 3418
Analogue Measure of Social Skills, 3970

Analytic Empathy Scale, 1370
Anaphora Test, 2370
Anger/Aggression Questionnaire, 7154
Anger Control Inventory, 5168
Anger Discomfort Scale, 7155
Anger Expression In and Out Scales, 5169
Anger Expression Scale, 7156
Anger Inventory, 2246, 3454, 3759, 5170 [See also Novaco Anger Inventory—Revised]
Anger Scales, 7157
Anger Self-Report, 2247, 3455
Anger Strain Scale, 7158
Anhedonia Scale, 910
Animal Empathy Scale, 6067
Animal Welfare Scale, 6068
Anomia Scale, Enlarged, 2563 [See also Srole Anomia Scale]
Anomie Index, 1640
Anomie Scale, 1078, 1091 [See also Srole Anomie Scale]
Anthropological Concept Attainment Test, 1269
Anti-Black Prejudice Scale, 2297
Anti-Black Racism Scale, 5715
Anticipated Shift in Self-Evaluation Scale, 6694
Anti-Democratic Attitude Instrument, 77
Anti-Industrial Values Scale, 3521
Anti-Semitism Scale, 5716
Antisexism Measure, 1123
Anti-White and Anti-Negro Scales, 46
Anti-White Racism Scale, 5717
Antonyms Test, 1904
Anxiety Differential, 2440
Anxiety Measure, 5457
Anxiety Questionnaire, 1641
Anxiety Scale, 2248, 3760–3762, 5215, 5458 [See also Costello-Comrey Anxiety Scale]
Anxiety Scale for Preschool Children, 1642
Anxiety Self-Rating Scale, 911

Anxiety Sensitivity Index, 5459
Anxiety Strain Scale, 5460
Anxiety-Stress Measure, 1643
Anxiety Symptom Checklist, 2441
Anxious Romantic Attachment Scale, 5461
Aphasia Screening Test—Partial, 5117
Aphasic Speech Evaluation Questions and Categories, 1887
Apparel Evaluation Scale, 7060
Applicant Attraction to the Organization Scale, 6535
Applicant Self-Report Interview Behavior, 6199
Applied Teaching Rating Scale, 7340
Appraisal Interview and Supervision Scale, 2036
Appraisal Interview Assessment Scale, 3162
Appraisal Scheme Scale, 1536
Appropriateness Checklist—Revised, 4757
Arabic Children's Depression Inventory, 5462
Arbitration Procedure Questionnaire, 1247
Are You Someone Who?, 1511
Areas of Change Questionnaire, 2966
Argumentativeness Scale, 3456
Argumentativeness Scales, 7159
Arithmetic Reasoning Test, 2204
Arizona Clinical Interview Rating Scale, 2330
Arlin Test of Formal Reasoning, 3419
Aronson Graphic Expression Scale, 715
Arousal Predisposition Scale, 6200
Arousal Seeking Tendency Scale—II, 6632
Arrow-Dot Task, 2158
Art and Music Activities Scale, 1841
Art Self-Perception Inventory, 6695

Articulation of the Body-Concept Scale, 4758
Articulation Survey, 3163
Artistic and Scientific Activity Survey, 6201
Ascription of Responsibility Questionnaire, 5025
Aspects of Identity Questionnaire, 4759
Aspects of Married Life Questionnaire, 6389
Assertion Inventory, 3457, 5171, 5172 [See also Gambrill-Richey Assertion Inventory]
Assertion Scale, 1702
Assertive Friend Cartoon Test, 2803
Assertive Job-Hunting Survey, 3458, 7160
Assertiveness Inventory, 7161
Assertiveness Rating Instrument, 2249
Assertiveness-Responsiveness Measure, 5173
Assertiveness Schedule, 7162 [See also Rathus Assertiveness Schedule]
Assertiveness Self-Report Inventory, 3459
Assessment of Career Decision Making, 2205, 2206
Assessment of Career Decision-Making, Decision-Making Style Scale, 3425
Assessment of Career Decision-Making Scale, 3610, 5118
Assessment of Career Decision Making—Styles Scale, 5306
Assessment Rating Profile, 6536
Associative Verbal Encoding, 1035
At-Risk Survey, 6052
AT-20, 5216 [See also Ambiguity Tolerance Scale; Intolerance of Ambiguity...; Revised Scale for Ambiguity Tolerance; Scale of Tolerance-Intolerance of Ambiguity; Tolerance for Ambiguity...]

Attachment Interview Q-Set, 7267
Attachment Q-Set, 5404, 6390
Attachment Scale, 5718
Attachment to Parents Scale, 6391
Attainment-Satisfaction Scale, 714
Attention Checklist, 4351
Attention to Body Shape Scale, 6696
Attitude-Behavior Scale, 1745
Attitude Functions Inventory, 4234
Attitude Measure of Sexual Behavior, 1747
Attitude of Concept—Educational Research, 1746
Attitude of the Gifted toward the Gifted Questionnaire, 1124
Attitude-Personality Questionnaire, 912
Attitude Questionnaire, 82, 1748
Attitude Research Instrument, 6069
Attitude Scale, 1749
Attitude Scale—LG, 6072
Attitude Survey, 150, 1125 [See also Survey of Attitude]
Attitude to Relationships Scale, 6392
Attitude toward Academic Acceleration of the Gifted Scale, 4261
Attitude toward Aggression Scale, 2706
Attitude toward Capital Punishment Scale, 1750
Attitude toward Change and Dissent Instrument, 484
Attitude toward Change Scale, 1129
Attitude toward Christianity Scale, 6095
Attitude toward College Inventory, 2692
Attitude toward Computer Usage Scale (Revised), 4237
Attitude toward Computers Scale—Hebrew Version, 6096
Attitude toward Contemporary Issues Questionnaire, 485
Attitude toward Controversy Scale, 2707

Attitude toward Counseling Scale, 2708

Attitude toward Disabled Persons Scale, 1751

Attitude toward Dreams Scale, 2709

Attitude toward Educational Inquiry, 2710

Attitude toward Educational Research Scale, 1752

Attitude toward Evangelism Scale, 2711

Attitude toward Expressing Feelings Survey, 1753

Attitude toward Full-Service Restaurants Scale, 4262

Attitude toward Human Resource Management Innovation, 4263

Attitude toward Instruction Scale, 2712

Attitude toward Instructional Television Scale, 488

Attitude toward Love Scale, 4264

Attitude toward Male Homosexuality Scale, 2713

Attitude toward Managing Work and Child Care, 4265

Attitude toward Materialism Scale, 6097

Attitude toward Negroes Rating Scale, 79

Attitude toward Nonmaternal Care Rating, 2967

Attitude toward Old People Scale, 1760

Attitude toward Physical Activity Inventory, 7211 [See also Kenyon Attitude toward Physical Activity Scale]

Attitude toward Psychiatric Patients Scale, 489

Attitude toward Public Exposure to Sexual Stimuli Scale, 1761

Attitude toward Rearing Adolescents—Q Sort, 490

Attitude toward Recycling Scale, 6098

Attitude toward Retail Bargaining Scale, 1762

Attitude toward School Questionnaire, 155

Attitude toward School Scale, 491, 4266

Attitude toward Science Scale, 4267

Attitude toward Self-Control Scale, 2714

Attitude toward Statistics Scale, 4268

Attitude toward Subject—Weighted or Conventional Multiple Choice Tests, 1453

Attitude toward Talented Youth Mathematics Program, 6099

Attitude toward Teaching as a Career Scale, 4269, 7355

Attitude toward Teaching Questionnaire, 492

Attitude toward Teaching Scale, 2716

Attitude toward the Church, 80

Attitude toward the Questionnaire Scale, 6100

Attitude toward Traditional/ Nontraditional Values Semantic Differential, 493

Attitude toward Treatment of Disabled Students Scale, 2717

Attitude toward War Scale, 6101

Attitude toward Women Scale, 4270

Attitude towards Christianity, 7213

Attitudes about Guilt Survey, 6070

Attitudes about Reality Scale, 4235, 6071

Attitudes Interview (Racial), 78

Attitudes of Elementary Teachers Questionnaire, 2691

Attitudes Questionnaire, 494

Attitudes to Females' Social Roles Questionnaire, 1755

Attitudes toward AIDS Scale—High School Version, 6087

Attitudes toward AIDS Victims Scale, 4236

Attitudes toward Applied Psychology Scales, 1127
Attitudes toward Birth Control Scale, 1128
Attitudes toward Censorship Scale, 6088
Attitudes toward Cheating Scale, 6073
Attitudes toward Christianity Scale, 4259
Attitudes toward College Courses, 151
Attitudes toward Computer-Assisted Instruction, 152
Attitudes toward Controversy Scale, 4238
Attitudes toward Cooperation Test, 1371
Attitudes toward Disabled Persons Scale, 2693, 6089
Attitudes toward Drug Usage and Drug Education Questionnaire, 1130
Attitudes toward Employee Drug Testing Scale, 6074
Attitudes toward Female Professors Scale, 1754
Attitudes toward Feminism and the Women's Movement Scale, 6075
Attitudes toward Feminism Scale, 4239
Attitudes toward Feminism Scale—Revised, 6076
Attitudes toward Financial Accounting, 4240
Attitudes toward Forcible Date Rape Scale, 6077
Attitudes toward Foreign Language Scale, 6078
Attitudes toward Fraternity Activities Questionnaire, 486
Attitudes toward Grading Questionnaire, 487
Attitudes toward Homosexuality Scale, 4241

Attitudes toward Individualized Education Program Measure, 6079
Attitudes toward Legalized Abortion Scale, 1131
Attitudes toward Lesbians and Gay Men, 6080
Attitudes toward Lesbians and Gay Men Scale—Revised, 4242
Attitudes toward Mainstreaming Scale, 2694
Attitudes toward Male Nurses Survey, 4243
Attitudes toward Marijuana Questionnaire, 1133
Attitudes toward Marijuana Scale, 1132
Attitudes toward Marriage Scale, 4244
Attitudes toward Married Professional Women Scale, 1134
Attitudes toward Masculine Transcendence Scale, 1757
Attitudes toward Mathematics, 153
Attitudes toward Mathematics—Revised, 1758
Attitudes toward Mathematics Scale, 2715
Attitudes toward Men Scale, 4245
Attitudes toward Mentally Retarded Children Scale, 1759
Attitudes toward Military Service, 81
Attitudes toward Nationalities, 1135
Attitudes toward Nuclear Disarmament Scale (AND), 2695
Attitudes toward Nurses Scale, 2696
Attitudes toward Obesity, 6090
Attitudes toward Occupations Scale, 2700
Attitudes toward Old People, 2697
Attitudes toward Parental Leave Takers Scale, 6697
Attitudes toward Psychiatrists and the Insanity Defense Scale, 6081

Attitudes toward Psychological Reports and Services, 154

Attitudes toward Rape Questionnaire, 4246

Attitudes toward School Measure, 1136

Attitudes toward Seeking Professional Psychological Help Scale, 1137, 1764, 2698, 6082 [See also Fisher-Turner Attitudes toward Seeking ...]

Attitudes toward Seeking Professional Psychological Help Scale— Revised, 4247

Attitudes toward Sex Role Scale, 4248

Attitudes toward Sex Roles Scale, 2699, 7061

Attitudes toward Social Studies Test, 1138

Attitudes toward Speakers Scale, 1765

Attitudes toward Statistics, 2701, 4249, 6083 [See also Survey of Attitudes toward Statistics]

Attitudes toward Supernatural Phenomena Scale, 1139

Attitudes toward Teaching as a Career Scale, 1140

Attitudes toward Teaching Reading in Content Classrooms Scale, 1763

Attitudes toward the Academic Environment Questionnaire, 1126

Attitudes toward the Grievance System, 4250

Attitudes toward the Handicapped Scale, 1756, 2702

Attitudes toward Transporting Nuclear Waste, 6084

Attitudes toward Wife Abuse Scale, 4521

Attitudes toward Women Carpenters Scale, 4253

Attitudes toward Women Scale, 1766–1768, 2703, 4252, 4255, 4256, 6085, 6086, 6092, 6093, 7210

Attitudes toward Women Scale— Adapted, 2704

Attitudes toward Women Scale for Adolescents, 4260

Attitudes toward Women Scale— Japanese Version, 7063

Attitudes toward Women Scale— Short, 6094

Attitudes toward Women Scale— Short Form, 4251, 4257, 4258, 7062

Attitudes toward Women Scales, 4254

Attitudes toward Working Mothers Scale, 2705, 4522

Attitudes toward Youth Scale, 1141

Attitudes towards Christianity Scale, 7212

Attitudes towards Incest Scale, 6091

Attitudinal Militancy Scale, 6102

Attitudinal Test, 2718

Attraction Questionnaire, 3971

Attraction to Feedback Scale, 6336

Attraction to Group Scale, 5719

Attribute Rating Scale, 1372, 7268

Attributes of Intelligence Scales, 6698

Attribution Inference Coding System, 2804

Attribution Inventory, 6701

Attribution of Success or Failure Scale, 1373

Attribution Questionnaire, 3164

Attributional Style Questionnaire, 3165, 4760, 4761, 6699, 6700

Attributional Tendency Scale, 3166

Attributions for Abuse Scale, 6702

Attributions for Success Scale, 5895

Attributive Causation Questionnaire, 1960

Audience Anxiousness Scale, 2551

Audio-Visual Perception, 1

Auditory Analysis of Speech, 6337
Auditory Analysis Test, 1374
Auditory Blending Test, 1036
Auditory Segmentation Test, 1037
Auditory Selective Attention Test, 3667
Auditory-Visual Integration Performance Test, 1596
Auditory-Visual Rhythm Perception Test, 750
Aural Word Representation Test, 602
Australian Sex-Role Scale, 3167
Australian Work Ethic Scale, 7214
Author Recognition Test, 5369
Authoritarianism Scale, 2250, 7163
Authority Behavior Inventory (ABI), 2805, 4352, 4353
Autobiographical Cognitions Questionnaire, 6991
Autobiographical Data Booklet B, 1444
Autokinetic Test, 913
Automated Patient Behavior Checklist, 1205
Automatic Thoughts Inventory, 5119
Automatic Thoughts Questionnaire, 2442, 3763, 5463
Automatic Thoughts Questionnaire—Positive, 5464
Automatic Word Processing Task, 2927
Autonomic Perception Questionnaire—Revision, 6703
Autonomous and Social Achievement Values Test, 2298
Autonomous Learning Behavior Scale, 4762
Autonomy and Relatedness Inventory, 5720
Autonomy-Control Scale, 2806, 3168
Autonomy Scale, 3051, 4763, 6992
Autostereotype-Heterostereotype Scale, 3169

Availability of Resources Scale, 6537
Aviation and Flying Attitude Questionnaire, 1142
Avoidability Measure, 6202
Avoidance of Existential Confrontation Scale, 2443
Avoidance of Ontological Confrontation with Death Scale, 5465
Avoidance of the Ontological Confrontation of Death Scale, 2444
Avoidance of the Ontological Confrontation of Loneliness Scale, 1703, 2552
Awareness of Comprehension Failure Test, 3170
Awareness of Consequences Test, 885
Ayers Prognostic Test for Early Childhood Education, 71

B

Baby Behavior Questionnaire, 3345
Bakker Assertiveness-Aggressiveness Inventory, 1842
Balance Beam Test, 3420
Balanced Inventory of Desirable Responding, 3972, 4764, 5721
Baldwin Picture-Story Measure of Kindness Concept, 1270
Bales Interaction Analysis, Adaptation of, 427
BAMED Teacher Rating Form, 5405
Bank Switching Questionnaire, 1308
Bank Teller Job Performance and Effectiveness Scale, 1537
Banking Attitude Questionnaire, 156
Barber Suggestibility Scale, 279, 914

Bargaining of Job-Related Issues Scale, 2719

Barnett Liking of Children Scale, 4271

Barrett Impulsiveness Scale, 6993 [See also Impulsiveness Scale]

Barrett-Lennard Relationship Inventory, 227, 309, 431, 1538, 2037, 2899, 3973, 4765, 5256, 7269 [See also Relationship Inventory]

Barrett-Lennard Relationship Inventory, Empathy Scale—OS Form, 5204

Barrett-Lennard Relationship Inventory, Form OS-64, Empathic Understanding Subscale, 3475

Barrett-Lennard Relationship Inventory—Revised, 2900, 2901, 5257, 7270

Barrett-Lennard Relationship Inventory (Short), 3974

Barriers to Marital Dissolution Scale, 2968

Barth Scale, 2038

Baseball Knowledge Test, 3668, 5370

Bases of Power Questionnaire, 52

Basic Mathematics Test, 2371

Basic Occupational Literacy Test, 1038

Basic Personality Inventory, 3346

Basic Reading Rate Scale, 1039

Basic Statistics Test, 2372

Battery of Interpersonal Capabilities, 7164

Bayley Mental Scale, 134

Bean Symbol Substitution Test, 340

Beauty Rating Scale, 751

Beck Anxiety Inventory, 3764, 5466

Beck Depression Inventory, 1644, 1645, 2445, 3769

Beck Depression Inventory—Abridged, 2446

Beck Depression Inventory (Dutch Version), 3768

Beck Depression Inventory—Modified, 3767

Beck Depression Inventory (Persian Version), 3766

Beck Depression Inventory—Short Form, 3765 [See also Depression Inventory (Short Form)]

Beck Hopelessness Scale, 3770 [See also Hopelessness Scale]

Becker Semantic Differential, 2251

Beginning Supervisor's Problems Questionnaire, 996

Behavior and Symptom Identification Scale (BASIS-32), 5467

Behavior Checklist, 1843, 3347

Behavior Codes for Job Environment, 3052

Behavior Description Referral Form, 388

Behavior Evaluation Rating Scale, 6209

Behavior Maturity Scale, 621

Behavior Orientation Card Sort, 228

Behavior-Problem Checklist, 1844, 2807 [See also Revised Behavior Problem Checklist]

Behavior Problems Questionnaire, 389

Behavior Profile, 716

Behavior Questionnaire, 6210

Behavior Rating Form, 1845, 2039

Behavior Rating Index for Children, 2808

Behavior Rating Scale, 5260, 6211

Behavioral Acculturation Scale—Adapted, 3975

Behavioral Acculturation Scale—Vietnamese, 5722

Behavioral Assertiveness Test, 3461

Behavioral Characteristics Rating Scale for Superior Students, 6203 [See also Scale for Rating Behavioral Characteristics of Superior Students]

Behavioral Checklist, 4354

Behavioral Correlates Scale—
Revised, 4766
Behavioral Dimensions Rating
Scale, 4355
Behavioral Expectation Scales,
2331
Behavioral Indecision Scale, 2809
Behavioral Index of Troubled
Employees, 4272
Behavioral Intentions Scale, 5896,
6204, 6205
Behavioral Interaction Measure,
585
Behavioral Inventory of Interper-
sonal Skills, 432
Behavioral Maturity Scale, 1206,
1937
Behavioral Objective Writing Skills
Test, 341
Behavioral Observation Scale, 6206
Behavioral Observation Scale—
Adapted, 5258
Behavioral Observation Scales,
2332, 3560
Behavioral Observation System,
1207
Behavioral Problems Index, 6207
Behavioral Problems Inventory and
Treatment Sheet, 495
Behavioral Rating Scale, 4356, 5259
Behavioral Rating Scales, 2810
Behavioral Role-Play Test, 4357
Behavioral Self-Report of Feminin-
ity, 6208, 7064
Behavioral Self-Report of Masculin-
ity Questionnaire, 7065
Behavioral Style Questionnaire,
1846, 2811
Behavioral Style Rating Scale, 564
Behavioral Styles Questionnaire,
3348
Behavioral Survey of Mentor
Behavior, 7271
Behavioroid Internal-External
Scale, 3171
Belcher Extended Loneliness Scale,
1704

Belief in a Just World, 3522
Belief in Lunar Effects Scale, 3172
Belief in Personal Control Scale,
4767
Belief in the Integrity of Man Scale,
915
Belief in the Paranormal Scale,
6103
Belief Questionnaire, 6994
Belief Systems Test, 4492
Belief that Change Can Be Effected
Scale, 6110
Beliefs about Academic Accelera-
tions Scale, 6104
Beliefs about Advertising Scale,
6105
Beliefs about Attractiveness
Questionnaire, 7215
Beliefs-about-Behavior Inventory,
1847
Beliefs about Consciousness and
Reality Scales, 6106
Beliefs about Equal Rights Scale,
2299
Beliefs about the Causes of Success
Scale—Classroom, 6107
Beliefs about the Causes of Success
Scale—Sport, 6108
Beliefs about the Consequences of
Maternal Employment for
Children, 4523
Beliefs and Actions Inventory, 4496
Beliefs and Fears Scale, 3462
Beliefs Regarding How One Reads
and How Reading Develops
Scale, 6109
Bell Global Psychopathology Scale,
3771, 5468
Bell Object Relations Inventory,
3772 [See also Object Relations
Inventory]
Bell Object Relations-Reality
Testing Inventory, 6995 [See also
Object Relations and Reality
Testing Inventory]
Bell Reality Testing Inventory,
3173

Belongingness Scales, 5723

Bem Sex Role Inventory, 2176, 3389

Bene-Anthony Family Relations Test, 141

Berger Sentence Completion Test, 752

Betts QMI Vividness of Imagery Scale, 753

Betts Questionnaire upon Mental Imagery—Revised, 6704 [See also Mental Imagery Questionnaire; Questionnaire upon Mental Imagery—Revised]

Betts-Sheehan Questionnaire upon Mental Imagery, 2040

Betts' Vividness of Imagery Scale, 1375 [See also Vividness of Imagery Scale]

Bialer-Cromwell Children's Locus of Control Scale, 754

Bialer-Cromwell Locus of Control Scale, 6705

Bialer Scale for Children, 2041

Bias in Attitude Survey Scale, 2720

Bicultural Involvement Questionnaire—Modified, 5724

Bieri Cognitive Complexity-Simplicity Scale, 433

Bieri Grid, 3421 [See also Kelly's Role Construct Repertory Test, Bieri's Modification of; Role Construct Repertory Test—Grid Form]

Big Five, 7054

Bills Index of Adjustment and Values, 300 [See also Index of Adjustment and Values]

Bills Junior High School Index of Adjustment and Values, 3523

Biodata Form, 6996

Biographical and Experience Questionnaire—Revised, 3773

Biographical Data Inventory, 839

Biographical Information Blank, 1445

Biographical Information Form, 212

Biographical Inventory, Adult I, 840

Biographical Inventory for the Arts, 2159

Biographical Inventory Questionnaire, 213

Biographical Questionnaire, 229, 1446, 3349, 5026

Biophilia Scale, 3524

Bipolar Adjective Scale, 6997

Bi-Polar Traits Inventory, 755

Black Ethnocentrism Scale, 3976

Black History Curriculum Priorities Rating, 157

Black Identification Scale, 5725

Black Racial Identity Attitude Scale, 5726

Black Racial Identity Attitude Scale—Form B, 5727

Black Separatism Scale, 3977

Black-White Interactions Attitude Scale, 1143

Blacks in Business Scale, 6111

Blake-Mouton Conflict Instrument, 1848

Blass Subjectivity-Objectivity Scale, 1769

Bledsoe Self Concept Scale, 1376

Block Child-Rearing Practices Report Q-Sort, 4524

Block Counting Test, 2042

Blomberg-Erickson-Lowery Computer Attitudes Task, 3774

Blood Donor Identity Scale, 4768

Blood Donor Salience Scale, 3174

Blood Donor Scales, 3978

Blumberg Supervisor Interaction System, 1248

Bodden Measure of Vocational Cognitive Complexity, 707

Bodily Feeling Scale, 4769

Body and Self Satisfaction Test, 756

Body Awareness Questionnaire, 4770, 6706

Body Cathexis, 2043

Body-Cathexis Scale, 4771, 6707

Body Cathexis Scale—Greek Version, 6708

Body Cathexis Scale—Modified, 3175, 4773, 4774
Body Cathexis Scale—Revised, 4772
Body-Consciousness Inventory, 4775
Body Consciousness Questionnaire, 4776
Body Distortion Questionnaire, 4273
Body-Esteem Scale, 3176, 6709
Body Esteem Scale—Female Subscales, 4777
Body-Image Assessment Scale, 6710
Body Image Avoidance Questionnaire, 6711
Body-Image Ideals Questionnaire, 6712
Body Image Questionnaire, 6713
Body Image Satisfaction Scale, 2044
Body Image Scale, 6714
Body Parts Satisfaction Questionnaire—Revised, 4779
Body Parts Satisfaction Scale, 3177, 4778, 6715
Body Satisfaction Questionnaire, 6716
Body-Self Relations Questionnaire, 4780, 4781
Body-Self Relations Questionnaire—Short Form, 6717
Body Sensations Questionnaire, 2812
Bogardus Social Distance Scale—Modified, 1144 [See also Social Distance Scale, Revised]
Borderline Syndrome Index, 3776
Boredom in Driving Scale, 3561
Boredom Proneness Scale, 3775, 5469
Borgotta Adherence to Authority Scale, 916
Bortner Rating Scale, 7165
Bortner Scale—Revised, 5174
Botel Reading Inventory, 2

Boundary-Spanning Roles Questionnaire, 3053
Boyar's Fear of Death Scale, 2447
Bradley Loneliness Scale, 1705
Bradley Loneliness Scale—Modified, 2553
Brainstorming Stress Scale, 5470
Branch Bank Climate for Service Survey, 3054
Brand Emotions Scale for Writers, 5027
Brayfield-Rothe Index, 1575
Brazelton Cambridge Newborn Scales, 1284
Brazelton Neonatal Behavioral Assessment Scale, 1849
Brazilian Health Locus of Control Scale, 6718
Brehem and Black Drug Attitude Scale, 1145
Breskin Nonverbal Rigidity Test, 1477
Breskin Rigidity Test, 917, 1377, 5175 [See also Rigidity Test]
Breznitz and Kugelmass Intentionality Questionnaire, 622
Brief Locus of Control Scale, 3178 [See also Locus of Control Scale—Brief Version]
Brief Psychiatric Rating Scale, 405, 1079
Brief Reasons for Living Inventory, 5471 [See also Reasons for Living Inventory]
Brief Symptom Inventory, 2448, 3777, 5472
Bristol Social Adjustment Guide, 6212
Brookover's Self-Concept of Ability Scale, 1850 [See also Self-Concept of Ability Scale]
Brown Locus of Control Scale, 4782
Bryan's Student Opinion Questionnaire—Revised, 997 [See also Student-Opinion Questionnaire]
Bulimia Cognitive Distortions Scale, 4783

Bulimia Test, 2813, 4358, 6213 [See also BULIT]
BULIT, 4359 [See also Bulimia Test]
Burden Assessment Scale, 5728
Burden Scale—Brief Version, 5729
Bureaucracy Scale, 1309
Bureaucratic/Employee Orientation Scale, 918
Bureaucratic Orientation Scale, 6112
Burnout Inventory, 5897
Burnout Measure, 2619
Buss Durkee Hostility Inventory, 2252, 3463, 6998 [See also Hostility Inventory]
Buss-Durkee Hostility Scale, 919
Buss-Durkee Inventory, 920
Buys' Scale of Attitude toward Contemporary Social Issues, 1146
Byrne Attraction Scale, Abridged, 426
Byrne Repression-Sensitization Scale, 921 [See also Repression-Sensitization Scale]

C

C-Scale, 1706
Calculator Attitude Scale, 2721
Caldwell Inventory of Home Stimulation, 2969 [See also Inventory of Home Stimulation]
California Child Q-Set, 1851
California F-Scale, 2253, 5176, 5177
Campbell-Kagan-Krathwohl Empathy Scale (Form B), 757
Campus Climate Survey, 6538
Campus Environment Survey, 6539
Campus Freedom-of-Expression Scale, 586
Canadian Readiness Test, 4223
Canadian Self-Esteem Inventory for Adults, 2046, 3179

Canadian Self-Esteem Inventory for Children, 2045, 6719
Cancer Inventory of Problem Situations, 3778
Cancer Locus of Control Scale (English Version), 4784
Cancer Perceived Self-Efficacy Scale, 4785
Cantril Time Perspective Scale, 758
Cantril's Self-Anchoring Striving Scale, 2047 [See also Self-Anchoring Striving Scale]
Card Rotation Test, 2048
Career Activities Survey, 2814
Career and Educational Self-Efficacy Scale, 6720
Career Attitude Scale, 6721
Career Choice Anxiety, 5898
Career Commitment Measure, 7356
Career Commitment Scale, 3611, 3612, 5307, 5308, 7357–7359
Career Concern Inventory—Adult Form, 5309
Career Counseling Diagnostic Inventory, 7360
Career Counselor Work Activity Questionnaire, 7272
Career Decision-Making Question-naire, 3613, 5310
Career Decision-Making Self-Efficacy Scale, 3180, 5311, 6722–6724
Career Decision Profile, 7361, 7362
Career Decision Scale, 2207, 7363
Career-Enhancing Strategies Scale, 7364
Career Exploration Scale, 7365
Career Exploration Survey, 3614, 5312, 5314, 7366
Career Exploration Survey—Adapted, 5313
Career Factor Checklist, 2360
Career Factors Inventory, 5315, 7367
Career Impatience Scale, 4119
Career Importance Scale, 5222, 7368

Career Indecision Factors Survey, 3615
Career Indecision Scale, 2208, 5316
Career Information-Seeking Scale, 3616
Career Insight Scale, 6725
Career Locus of Control Scale, 4786, 6726
Career Motivation Study, 7369
Career Myths Scale, 6727
Career Orientation Inventory, 3617
Career Orientation Scale, 1576, 3618
Career Pattern Study Work Values Inventory—Adapted, 708
Career Planning Questionnaire, 3619, 5317
Career Planning Scale, 5318
Career Preferences Scales, 5319
Career Reading Appreciation Form, 7066
Career-Related Concerns Checklist, 5899
Career Salience Questionnaire, 2235, 3620
Career Salience Scale, 3621, 5900, 5901
Career Satisfaction Scale, 5902, 5903
Career Search Self-Efficacy Scale, 6728
Career Self-Efficacy Expectations Scale, 6729
Career Self-Efficacy Scale, 6730–6732
Career Strategy Scale, 4120
Career Support Scale—Modified, 7273
Career Transition Inventory, 5904
Career Values Scale, 5223
Career Withdrawal Cognitions Scale, 7370
Career Withdrawal Intentions Scale, 5905
Caregiver Dislocations Scale, 5730
Caregiver Support Appraisal Scale—P, 6393

Caregiver Support Appraisal Scale—V, 6394
Caregiver Supportive Behavior, 7274
Carey Scale, Revised, 2285
Carey Survey of Temperamental Characteristics, 2254
Carkhuff's Discrimination Indexes, 1249
Carleton University Responsiveness to Suggestion Scale (CURSS), 2902
Carpenter Apprentice Program Questionnaire, 4634
Catastrophic Cognitions Question-naire—Modified, 5473
Categories Test, 1147
Categorization Behavior Test, 623
Category System for Partners Interaction, 4525
Category Width Questionnaire, 1271
Cattell-Curran Psychological State Battery, 841
Catterall-Reece, Ipsative, True-Ideal, Q-Sort, Upper Elementary Test—Revised, 759
Causal Construct Scale, 2177
Causal Dimension Scale, 3181, 4787
Causal Dimension Scale—Modified, 5178
Causality Test, 886
Celebrity Appeal Questionnaire, 5731
Center for Epidemiologic Studies Depression Scale, 2449, 3779, 3780, 5474–5477 [See also Depression Scale]
Central Life Interest Scale, 2361
Central Life Interests Question-naire—Modified, 3622
Certainty of Occupational Prefer-ence Scale, 3623

Chabassol Adolescent Structure Inventory, 760, 1378, 1991 [See also Adolescent Structure Inventory]

Chairmanship Functions Questionnaire, 657

Chance Scale, 4788 [See also Levenson Internal, Powerful Others, and Chance Scales]

Chance Self-Report Scale, 6733

Chaney Short Form Vocational Values Inventory, 1512

Change Scale, 624

Change Seeker Index, 717, 1992

Changes in Self-Perception Scale, 2970

Characteristics of a Treatment Environment Instrument, 1310

Characteristics of Client Growth Scale, 1646

Characteristics of Lifelong Learners in the Professions, 4121

Cheating Attitude Questionnaire, 4274

Cheating Questionnaire, 6214

Cheating Test, 922

Checklist of Interpersonal Transactions—Revised, 5732

Checklist of Perceptual-Motor and Language Skills, 1597

Checklist of Physical Limitations, 3781

Checklist of Positive and Negative Thoughts, 2402

Checklist of Positive and Negative Thoughts—Modified, 2403

Cherniss Burnout Measure, 5906

Chicago Activity Inventory, 1707

Child Abuse Potential Inventory, 2815, 3350

Child Abuse Potential Inventory, Inconsistency Scale, 4395

Child Abuse Potential Inventory, Lie Scale, 2846

Child Behavior Checklist, 4360

Child Behavior Checklist, Ages 2–3, 6215 [See also Achenbach Child Behavior Checklist]

Child Behavior Inventory, 496

Child Behavior Profile—Teacher Version, 2816

Child Behavior Rating Scale, 28, 2945, 4361

Child Behavior toward the Parent Inventory, 4526

Child Behaviors Inventory of Playfulness, 4362

Child-Care Problem Scale, 4527

Child Development Questionnaire, 625

Child Rating Questionnaire, 6216

Child Rating Scale, 4528

Child-Rearing Beliefs Scales, 6113

Child-Rearing Questionnaire, 1148

Child Report: School Attitude Scale, 1149

Child Stimulus Screening Scale, 1852, 3351

Child Study Inventory, 1945

Child-Study Team Conflict Questionnaire, 1466

Child Temperament Questionnaire, 2817

Childhood Depression Inventory, 5478

Childhood Obesity Scale, 6734

Childhood Social Network Questionnaire, 3979

Children of Alcoholics Life Events Schedule, 6395

Children of Alcoholics Screening Test, 6396

Children's Ability-Effort Scale, 3782

Children's Academic Anxiety Inventory, 2404

Children's Academic Coping Inventory, 3697

Children's Academic Intrinsic Motivation Inventory, 3127

Children's Academic Motivation Inventory, 4699

Children's Action Tendency Scale, 3464, 4363, 4364

Children's Apperception Test (CAT), Puzzle Form, 1450

Children's Assertive Behavior Scale, 3465, 4365

Children's Associative Responding Test, 264

Children's Attitude toward Authority Scale, 2723

Children's Attitudes toward Handicapped Scale, 4275

Children's Attitudes toward Institutional Authority Scale, 6114

Children's Attitudes toward Television Commercials, 2722

Children's Attitudinal Range Indicator, 497

Children's Attributional Style Questionnaire, 4789

Children's Authoritarian Personality Scale, 3466

Children's Beliefs about Parental Divorce Scale, 4529

Children's Coercive Behavior Scale, 2818

Children's Cognitive Assessment Questionnaire, 2405

Children's Conservatism Scale, 1513

Children's Depression Inventory, 2450, 3783

Children's Depression Scale, 5479

Children's Divorce Adjustment Scale, 4530

Children's Drug-Use Survey, 2819

Children's Friendship Expectancy Inventory, 5733

Children's Handwriting Scale, 2373

Children's Hostility Inventory, 5179

Children's Intent Judgment Rating Scale, 626

Children's Intervention Rating Profile, 4366

Children's Locus of Control Scale, 3182

Children's Locus of Evaluation and Control Scale, 2049

Children's Loneliness Scale, 2554

Children's Manifest Anxiety Scale, 1478 [See also Manifest Anxiety Scale, Children's Form]

Children's Manifest Anxiety Scale, Revised, 2524 [See also Revised Children's Manifest Anxiety Scale]

Children's Minimal Social Behavior Scale (CMSBS), 842

Children's Negative Cognitive Error Questionnaire, 3784

Children's Occupation, Activity, and Trait-Attitude Measure, 6115

Children's Own Perceptions and Experiences of Stressors, 3184

Children's Paced Auditory Serial Addition Task, 7119

Children's Perceived Control Scale, 4790

Children's Perceived Self-Control Scale, 3185

Children's Perception Questionnaire, 4531

Children's Perceptions of Everyday Schooling Conventions, 3055

Children's Perceptions of Parents Scale, 6397

Children's Personal Attributes Inventory, 3186

Children's Personal Attributes Questionnaire—Short Form, 5028

Children's Pictorial Attitude Scale, 1770

Children's Practices Inventory, 6540

Children's Problem-Solving Skills Measure, 5120

Children's Reinforcement Survey Schedule, 1853

Children's Report of Parental Behavior Inventory, 6398

Children's Responsibility Inventory, 762

Children's Role Inventory, 6399
Children's Scale of Social Attitudes, 4276
Children's School Questionnaire, 843
Children's School-Related Attitudes Self-Report Questionnaire, 1771
Children's Self-Concept Index, 763
Children's Self-Control Scale, Self-Control Subscale, 6900
Children's Self Description Questionnaire, 4791
Children's Self-Efficacy for Peer Interaction Scale, 3980, 4792
Children's Self-Perception Scale, 3187
Children's Self-Social Construct Test, 434
Children's Sex-Role Test, 3188
Children's Social Desirability Questionnaire, 1708, 5734
Children's Social Desirability Scale, 435
Children's Social Support Scale, 3981
Children's Somatization Inventory, 5480
Children's Sport Goal Orientation Inventory, 6633
Child's Learning Ability Rating Scale, 2677
Child's Report of Parental Behavior Inventory, 2971
Child's Report of Parental Behavior—Revised, 761
Child's Self-Concept, 230
Choice Dilemma Questionnaire, 2160, 2255
Choice Dilemmas Questionnaire, Revised, 2161
Choice-Monitor Scale, 3390
Christianity Orthodoxy Scale, 7216
Chronic Disease Impression Rating Scales, 4794
Chronic Self-Destructiveness Scale, 5481, 6217
Chronicity of Loneliness Scale, 3982

Cincinnati Autonomy Test Battery, 658, 1208
Circadian Type Scales, 7166
Circle Reasoning Test, 2209
Civil-Liberties Climate Scale, 4795
Clarity of Self Concept Semantic Differential, 1379
Clark Doll Test, 1150
Clarke Science Interest Checklist, 864
Class Activities Questionnaire, 1380
Class Atmosphere Scale, 2050
Class Attendance Survey, 3698
Class Consciousness Scale, 3189
Class Involvement Measure, 5406
Class Play, 1695 [See also Revised Class Play]
Classification and Seriation Test, 2946
Classification Skills Development Test, 627
Classroom Adjustment Rating Scale, 2820
Classroom Adjustment Scale, 2406
Classroom and Social Involvement Scales, 3699
Classroom Behavior Inventory, 565, 718, 1854, 1993, 6218 [See also Schaefer Classroom Behavior Inventory]
Classroom Behavior Inventory, Preschool to Primary, 390 [See also Schaefer Classroom Behavior Inventory]
Classroom Behavior Observation, 2821
Classroom Behavior Rating Scale, 1855
Classroom Behavior Rating Scales, 566
Classroom Behavior Scale, 3056
Classroom Environment Index, 3057
Classroom Environment Scale— Form D, 1539

Classroom Inappropriate Behavior Scale, 2822
Classroom Interaction Analysis, 2823
Classroom Life Instrument, 3058, 6219
Classroom Preference Test, 865
Classroom Procedures Evaluation Form, 7275
Classroom Status and Teacher Approval-Disapproval Question-naire, 659
Classroom Test of Formal Reason-ing, 7120
Claustrophobia General Cognitions Questionnaire, 5482
Claustrophobia Situations Ques-tionnaire, 5483
Clerical Job Condition and Task Preference Schedule, 2178
Client & Therapist Perceptions of Own & Other's Problem Solving Adequacy, 764
Client Assessment Questionnaire, 1080
Client Attachment to Therapist Scale, 7276
Client Attitude Questionnaire, 1772
Client Beliefs Inventory, 3190
Client Change Inventory, 7277
Client Evaluation of Counselor Scale, 7278
Client Expectancy Questionnaire, 3191
Client Fears Questionnaire, 2451
Client Personal Reaction Question-naire, 998
Client Rating Scale, 2903
Client Resistance Scale, 7279
Client Satisfaction Form, 5261
Client Satisfaction Questionnaire, 4636, 4637, 6541
Client Satisfaction Questionnaire—Short, 4635
Client Satisfaction Scale, 3059
Client Verbal Information Seeking Behavior System, 587

Client's Self-Rating Scale, 310
Cline Interpersonal Film Tests, 765
Clinical Anxiety Scale, 3785
Clinical Anxiety Scale (French), 5484
Clinical Assessment Inventory, 2452
Clinton Assessment of Problem Identification Skills, 3562
Close Friendship Scale, 5735
Clothing Interest Scale, 7067
Clothing Values Inventory, 5224
Cloze Test—Modified, 1598
Cloze Tests, Two, 20
Coan Experience Inventory, 2162
Cockpit Management Attitudes Questionnaire—Revised, 4277
Code for Instructional Structure and Student Academic Response, 2824
Cognition and Reading Comprehen-sion Scales, 3669
Cognition Checklist, 5486
Cognition of Behavioral Units, 2555
Cognition of Semantic Implications Test, 266
Cognition of Semantic Transforma-tions Test, 106
Cognition of Semantic Units Test, 3
Cognition of Symbolic Transforma-tions Test, 107
Cognition of Symbolic Units Test, 108
Cognitions of Home Scale, 6400
Cognitive Achievement Battery on Scientific Literacy, 5371
Cognitive and Affective Computer Attitude Scales, 2724
Cognitive Anxiety Inventory—State, 5485
Cognitive Components System, 1209
Cognitive Contribution Test, 3563
Cognitive Error Questionnaire, 5029, 6735

Cognitive Error Questionnaire (General and Lower Back Pain Versions), 3192

Cognitive Error Questionnaire (Rheumatoid Arthritis Version), 3786

Cognitive Failures Questionnaire, 5121

Cognitive Flexibility Scale, 7167

Cognitive Flexibility Test, 923

Cognitive Home Environment Scale, 642, 1294

Cognitive Interference Questionnaire, 5122, 5487

Cognitive Laterality Questionnaire, 3422

Cognitive Preference Inventory, 1479

Cognitive Preference Reading Instrument, 3391

Cognitive Preference Test, 2179

Cognitive Process Inventory, 265

Cognitive Process Questionnaire, 3423

Cognitive Process Survey, 3193, 4796

Cognitive Skills Inventory, 5372

Cognitive Slippage Scale, 6220

Cognitive-Somatic Anxiety Questionnaire, 3787, 5180

Cognitive Status Examination, 5123

Cognitive Tasks, 2678

Cognitive Therapy Scale, 5262

Cognitive Triad Inventory, 3788, 5488

Cognitive Vocational Maturity Test, 1938

Cognitive Vocational Maturity Tests, 1040

Collaborative Study Psychotherapy Rating Scale, 5263

Colleague Teacher-Description Scales, 1541

Collective Bargaining Attitude Scale, 1773

Collective Bargaining Goals, 6542

Collectivism/Power Distance Measure, 5225

College Adaptation Scale—Participant, 3700

College Adjustment Inventory, 3701

College Admissions Assistance Questionnaire, 660

College Alumni Questionnaire, 158

College Business Major Curriculum Objectives Survey, 661

College Characteristic Index, 1311 [See also Stern's College Characteristics Index]

College Choice Influence Scale, 7068

College Classroom Environment Scales, 6543

College Course Evaluation Form, 1540

College Criteria Questionnaire, 1856

College Descriptive Index, 2407

College Dropout Self-Report Screening Inventory, 3702

College Expectations Questionnaire—Adapted, 662

College Interaction Self-Efficacy Questionnaire, 4797

College Inventory of Academic Adjustment, 22

College Major Prestige Questionnaire, 896

College Maladjustment Scale, 3703

College Opinion Survey, 231, 232, 766

College Optimism Scale, 2408

College Peer Rating System, 2556

College Performance Questionnaire, 5407

College Press and Attitude Scales, 1151

College Self-Expression Scale, 2256, 3467, 7168

College Self-Expression Scale (Spanish Version), 5181

College Student Academic Locus of Control Scale, 3194
College Student Drug Use Questionnaire, 1210
College Student Life Event Schedule, 3789, 5489
College Student Satisfaction Questionnaire, 159, 663, 1961
College Student Satisfaction Questionnaire—Revised, 3704
College Teacher-Description Scales, 2334
College Teaching Effectiveness Questionnaire, 1542, 2333
College Women's Assertion Sample, 3468, 5182
Collett-Lester Fear of Death Scale, 2453 [See also Fear of Death Scale]
Collett-Lester Fear of Dying Scale, 406
Collins Attitudes toward Computers Survey—Short Form, 4278
Color-a-Person Body Dissatisfaction Test, 6736
Color Meaning Test II, 1774
Color-Word Test, 924
Colorado Childhood Temperament Inventory, 3352
Combat Experience Scale, 6221
Combat Exposure Scale, 2825
Combat-Related Posttraumatic Stress Disorder Subscale, 2454
Comfortable Interpersonal Distance Scale, 436
Commitment Inventory, 6401
Commitment Scale, 3624 [See also Porter Commitment Scale]
Commitment to Career Choices Scale, 7371
Commitment to College Questionnaire, 206
Commitment to Physical Activity Scale, 5081
Commitment to the Union Scale, 5320, 5321, 7372 [See also Union Commitment Scale]

Common Ailments, 407
Common Belief Inventory for Students, 5124
Common Beliefs Survey III, 5125
Communication Quality Scale, 4479
Communication Satisfaction Questionnaire, 2904
Communication Scale, 2905
Communication Skills Test, 2972
Communicative Adaptability Scale, 6338
Communicative Egocentrism Scale, 1480
Community College Counselor Training Questionnaire, 664
Community College Motivation Inventory, 1994
Community Commitment Scale, 3983
Community Competence Scale, 4367
Community Competence Scale—Revised, 3791
Community Dental Health Ideology Scale, 2725
Community Judgment Scale, 1312
Community Organizational Scale, 1454
Community Satisfaction Scale, 4279
Community Satisfaction Scale—Revised, 3060
Companion Animal Bonding Scale, 3984
Companion Animal Semantic Differential, 4798, 5736
Companion Animal Semantic Differential—Short Form, 4799
Company Practices Scale, 6544
Company Satisfaction Scale, 4122
Competence Index, 4123
Competence Inventory for College Students, 2409
Competency Rating Scale, 6737
Competency Scale, 767
Competition Knowledge Test, 2826, 2928

Competitive-Cooperative Attitude
    Scale, 5183
Competitive-Cooperative Attitudes
    Scale, 1775
Competitive Sport Anxiety Inven-
    tory, 5490
Competitive State Anxiety Inven-
    tory-2, 3790, 5491
Competitiveness Index, 7169
Competitiveness Questionnaire,
    4700
Complacency Potential Rating
    Scale, 6738
Complexity Scale, 768
Complexity Self-Description Scale,
    1481
Compliance with Interviewer
    Requests Scale, 2906
Compliance with Supervisor's
    Wishes Scale, 6222
Complutense University Teachers
    Evaluation Questionnaire, 7280
Comprehension of Consent/Coercion
    Measure, 5737
Comprehension of Social-Moral
    Concepts Test, 1599, 2300
Comprehension Skills Test, 5
Comprehensive Job Evaluation
    Technique, 3061
Comprehensive Mathematics
    Inventory, 4
Comprehensive Social Desirability
    Scale for Children, 2557
Compulsive Eating and Dietary
    Concern with Weight Scales,
    4368
Compulsive Eating Scale, 4369
Computer-Aided Design Anxiety
    Questionnaire, 5907
Computer Anxiety Factor, 5908
Computer Anxiety Index, 3792
Computer Anxiety Rating Scale,
    3793, 5909, 5910
Computer Anxiety Scale, 3705,
    3794, 3795, 4280, 5911
Computer Aptitude Scale—Revised,
    4224

Computer Attitude Scale, 2726,
    2727, 4225, 4281–4283, 6116
Computer Attitude Scale (CATT),
    4284
Computer Attitude Scale (NCAS),
    4285
Computer Hassles Scale, 5912
Computer Playfulness Scale, 6223
Computer Rating Form, 7281
Computer-Related Attitudes Scale,
    2728
Computer-Related Beliefs Scale,
    2729
Computer Science Success Predictor
    Test, 2679
Computer Self-Efficacy Scale, 4800,
    6739, 6740
Computer Technology Hassles
    Scale, 3796, 3797, 5913
Concept Attainment Scale, 2929
Concept Definition and Application
    Test, 2930
Concept-Specific Anxiety Scale,
    1381, 1648
Concepts of Development Question-
    naire, 6371
Conceptual Level Analogy Test,
    3424
Conceptual Level Questionnaire,
    135
Conceptual Level Scale, 4493
Conceptual Pre-Structuring for
    Detailed Verbal Passages, 109
Conceptual Style Test (CST), 603,
    1272, 1905
Conceptual Style Test—Revised,
    1906
Concern about Teaching Scale, 4124
Concern for Appropriateness Scale,
    2558, 3985
Concern for Environmental Rights
    Scale, 1152
Concern over the Negative Conse-
    quences of Success Scale, 2455
Concern with Regard of Others
    Scale, 3986

Concerns about Computers Scale, 5914

Confidence in Child Management Scale, 2051

Confidence in Management Scale, 5264

Confidence Scale, 2907, 4801

Conflict Behavior Questionnaire, 4532, 6402

Conflict Resolution Inventory, 1857

Conflict Resolution Styles Inventory, 6403

Conflict Tactics Scales, 2973, 4626

Conflictual Independence Scale, 6404

Confucian Ethics Scale, 7217

Congregation Satisfaction Questionnaire, 3062

Conjugal Understanding Measure, 4533

Connecticut Needs Assessment Survey, 3195

Conners Teacher Rating Scale, 2827

Conners Teacher Rating Scale—Revised, 2828

Consensual Index, 100

Consequences of Working and Not Working Scale, 2730

Consequences Test, 1907, 1920

Conservatism Measure, 2257

Conservatism-Radicalism Opinionnaire, 280

Conservatism Scale, 1776, 1777, 2731

Conservatism Scale for Urban Afrikaners, 2732

Conservatism Scale—Short Form, 6117

Constriction Scale, 408

Constructive Thinking Scale, 7121

Consultant Evaluation Form, 7282

Consultation Judgment Inventory, 3670

Consumer Exchange Scale, 4370

Consumers' Susceptibility to Salespersons' Influence Scale, 6999

Consumption Experiences Scale, 2829

Contact with Medical Health Care Professionals Inventory, 6339

Contemporary Topics Questionnaire (CTQ), 498

Contemporary Work Ethic Scale, 7218

Content Analysis Scales of Psychosocial Maturity, 2947

Contextual Performance Scale, 5915

Contextual Uncertainty Scale, 2908

Contingent-Noncontingent Expectancy Scale, 3196

Continuance Commitment Scale, 3625, 5322, 5916, 7373, 7374 [See also Affective and Continuance Commitment Scale]

Continued Attachment Scale, 6405

Contraceptive Situations Questionnaire, 3987

Control of Imagery Questionnaire, 2052

Control Questionnaire, 1962

Control Scale, 6406

Controversy Attitude Scale, 2733

Conventionality Scale, 2734

Convergent Production of Semantic Transformations Test, 127

Convergent Production of Symbolic Transformations Test, 126

Cooperation Scales, 5917

Cooperative Attitude in School Settings Scale, 4371

Cooperative/Competitive Strategy Scale, 4286

Cooperativeness and Competitiveness Scale—Italian Version, 5738

Cooperativeness in Conflict Scale, 4534

Coopersmith Self-Esteem Inventory, 499, 2053, 2054, 3197 [See also Self-Esteem Inventory]

Coordinating Style Scale, 3988

COPE, 5492

Coping Analysis Schedule for Educational Settings, 1211

Coping-Health Inventory for Parents, 4535

Coping Humor Scale, 3798, 5493

Coping Inventory for Stressful Situations, 5494

Coping Orientation for Problem Experiences Scale, 3799

Coping Responses Scale, 5495

Coping Scale, 3800, 5323, 5496

Coping Strategies and Resources Inventory, 2974

Coping Strategies Inventory, 2830, 3801, 5497

Coping Strategies Questionnaire for SCD, 3802

Coping Strategies Scale, 5498

Coping Strategy Indicator, 5499

Coping Styles Questionnaire, 3803

Coping with Job Loss Scales, 4125

Coping with Separation Inventory— Revised, 2975

Cornell Parent Behavior Description, 643, 4536

Cornell Parent Behavior Inventory, 4537

Cornell Parenting Activities List, 4538

Correlation of Item-Examinee Sampling Procedures and Estimation of Test Parameters, 161

Costello-Comrey Anxiety Scale, 925 [See also Anxiety Scale]

Cottle School Interest Inventory, 391

Couch-Kiniston Agreement-Response Test, 281 [See also Agreement Response Scale]

Counseling and Religion Opinion Survey, 7219

Counseling Appropriateness Checklist, 409, 2909 [See also Warman's Counseling Appropriateness Checklist]

Counseling Attitude Scale— Revised, 4638

Counseling Center Questionnaire, 1313

Counseling Evaluation Inventory, 2335, 3063, 3564, 4639, 5266, 7283

Counseling Evaluation Questionnaire, 1000

Counseling Expectation Inventory, 3198

Counseling Information Scale, 2374

Counseling Outcome Measure, 3804, 4375

Counseling Outcome Questionnaire, 7284

Counseling Outcome Semantic Differential, 500

Counseling Performance Scale, 4640

Counseling Rating Form, 2336

Counseling Reaction Questionnaire, 311

Counseling Self-Estimate Inventory, 6741

Counseling Situations Inventory, 4701

Counseling Skills Rating Scale, 1543

Counselor Appraisal of Position Scale, 665

Counselor Behavior Evaluation Form, 3565

Counselor Competence Scale, 7285

Counselor Development Questionnaire, 3568

Counselor Education Program Innovation Index (CEPII), 160

Counselor Effectiveness Rating Scale, 3567, 5267–5269

Counselor Effectiveness Rating Scale—Modified, 7286

Counselor Effectiveness Scale, 312, 1001, 1002, 2337, 3566, 5270, 5271, 7287 [See also Rating Scale of Counselor Effectiveness]

Counselor Effectiveness Scale, Adaptation of, 307
Counselor Evaluation Inventory, 999, 3569, 4641, 5265
Counselor Evaluation of Supervisor Form—Modified, 7288
Counselor Evaluation Rating Scale, 2339, 3570, 5272, 7289
Counselor Expectancy Test, 1382
Counselor Function Inventory, 3199
Counselor Interview Competence Scale, 3571
Counselor Occupational Stress Inventory (COSI), 2620
Counselor Orientation Questionnaire, 2340
Counselor Perception Questionnaire, 3200
Counselor Practicum Evaluation Form, 1003
Counselor Preference Inventory, 7290
Counselor Preference Questionnaire, 3392
Counselor Preference Questionnaire—Revised, 7070
Counselor Preference Survey, 1544
Counselor R Scale, 2163
Counselor Rating Form, 2341, 2342, 3353, 3573, 4803, 5273, 7291, 7293
Counselor Rating Form—Short, 5274, 7292
Counselor Rating Form—Short Version, 3572
Counselor Response Questionnaire, 2343
Counselor Role Concepts Analysis, 313
Counselor Role Questionnaire, 314
Counselor Selection Instrument, 1004
Counselor Social Reinforcement and Persuasion Scales, 1545
Counselor Verbal Response Scale, 101, 588

Counselor's Facilitative Conditions Scales, 2344
Counselor's Self-Rating Scale, 769
Countertransference Factors Inventory, 7295
Countertransference Factors Inventory—Modified, 7294
Couple Therapy Alliance Scale, 2559, 5275
Course and Instructor Questionnaire, 1546
Course Evaluation Form, 666
Course Evaluation Instrument, 667, 2338
Course Evaluation Inventory, 1547
Course Evaluation Questionnaire, 668, 7296
Course Evaluation Scales, 3064
Course Rating Scale for Organizational Behavior, 3065
Course Structure Inventory, 2735
Courses Interest Inventory, 7069
Courtly Love Scale, 3989
Covert Thoughts Questionnaire, 3201
Co-Worker Commitment Scale, 3990
Crandall Locus of Control Instrument, 1383
Creative Activities Checklist, 2940, 4494
Creative Activity Questionnaire, 1921
Creative Behavior Check List for Disadvantaged Children, 1922
Creative Behavior Disposition Scale, 1923
Creative Motivation Scale, 607
Creative Product Semantic Scale, 4495
Creativity Battery, 1924
Creativity/Leadership Self-Rating Chart, 1925
Creativity Questionnaire, 1280
Creativity Styles Questionnaire, 6365
Creativity Test Battery, 6366

Credibility Checklist, 1888
Credibility Scale, 4372, 4373
Creech Mental Illness Question-
naire, 2736
Creedal Assent Index, 3525
Crime Victimization Locus of
Control Scale, 6742
Crisis Call Outcome Rating Scale,
4374
Criterion Group Elementary
Guidance Opinionnaire, 315
Critical Incident Counselor Ethical
Discrimination Ability Question-
naire, 969
Criticism Concerns Scale, 4804
Cross-Cultural Attitude Behavior
Scale, 1153
Cross-Cultural Competency Scale,
5276
Cross-Cultural Counseling Inven-
tory—Revised, 7297
Cross-Cultural World-Mindedness
Scale, 6118
Crowne-Marlowe Social Desirability
Scale, 48, 49 [See also Marlowe-
Crowne Social Desirability Scale;
Social Desirability Scale]
CSSB Rating Scale, 844
Cubes, 3671
Cue Count, 2456
Cue Interpretations Test, 1340
Cultural Alienation and Cultural
Commitment Scales, 1092
Cultural Knowledge Checklist, 5373
Cultural Mistrust Inventory, 2560,
3991, 5739
Cultural Participation Scale—Short
Form, 4642
Cultural Rating Scale for Homicide
Regulation, 970
Culture Fair Intelligence Test, 468
Curiosity Scale, 233
Curiosity Test, 1778
Current Life Orientation Scale,
7220
Current Mood State Scale, 2457

Current Sexual Activities Scale,
4376
Curriculum Attitude Inventory, 501
Curriculum Development Criteria,
1314
Curriculum Evaluation Question-
naire in Social Welfare, 162
Curriculum-People Semantic
Differential Scales, 502
Customer Satisfaction Scale, 7071
Customer Service-Related Practices
Survey, 3066
Cybernetics Attitude Scale, 4287
Cynical Distrust Scale, 5030, 5740

D

Dahlhauser Football Locus of
Control Scale, 4805
Daily Activity List, 567
Daily Assessment Form, 5500
Daily Child Behavior Checklist,
2831
Daily Hassles Questionnaire, 5501
Daily Hassles Scale, 5502
Dangerousness of Mental Patients
Scale, 4377
Daniels Word Recognition Test, 342
Data-Entry Stress Scale, 5918
Dating and Assertion Question-
naire, 3992, 3997 [duplicate],
7170
Dating Anxiety Survey, 3993
Dating Behavior Instrument, 4378
Dating Competence Scale, 5741
Dating Conflict Scale, 5742
Dating Interaction Scales, 5744
Dating-Marriage Scale, 503
Dating Motive Scale, 3128
Daydream Assessment Question-
naire, 3354
Daytime Sleepiness Scale, 6224
Dean's Alienation Scale, 437, 1093,
1709 [See also Alienation Scale]
Death Acceptance Scale, 2458

Death Anxiety Scale, 410, 1649–1651, 2459, 3805, 5503 [See also Templar Death Anxiety Scale]

Death Attitude Scale, 1779

Death Behavior Questionnaire, 5504

Death Concern Scale, 411, 1652, 2460, 3806

Debilitating Anxiety Scale, 3706

Decision Conflict and Cooperation Questionnaire, 4480

Decision Control Index, 4539

Decision-Difficulty Checklist, 2180

Decision Influence Measure, 4379

Decision Latitude Scale, 4643

Decision-Making Authority Scale, 7122

Decision Making Information Needs Questionnaire, 4702

Decision-Making Policy Scale, 2910

Decision-Making Questionnaire, 7123

Decisional Procrastination Scale, 6225

Deductive/Inductive Reasoning Tests, 3426

Defense Language Aptitude Battery, 1733

Defense Mechanism Inventory, 1653, 3355 [See also Gleser-Ihilevich Defense Mechanism Inventory]

Defense Mechanism Inventory—Adolescent Version Short Form, 7000

Defensive-Nondefensive Communication Behavior Rating Scale, 1250

Defensiveness Scale for Children, 5031

Deferment of Gratification Scale, 4703

Defining Issues Test, 1939, 2210, 2301, 3994, 5126

Degree of Tolerance Scales, 2258

Del Greco Assertive Behavior Inventory, 3469

Delay Tolerance Inventory, 1212

Delinquency Questionnaire, 1213

Delinquency Scale, 6226, 6227

Delinquency Scales, 2832

Democratic Deficiency Scale, 2055

Denial of Distress Scale, 5745

Departmental Commitment Questionnaire, 7375

Departmental Quality Scale, 3067

Dependence-Independence Scales, 282

Dependence Proneness Scale, 4380

Depersonalization Scale, 7001

Depression and Irritation Scales, 2621

Depression-Happiness Scale, 5505

Depression Index, 5506

Depression Inventory (Short Form), 1654 [See also Beck Depression Inventory—Short Form]

Depression Locus of Control Scale, 4806, 4807

Depression Measure, 3807

Depression Proneness Rating Scale, 2462, 3808, 5507

Depression Scale, 2463, 2464, 5508–5510 [See also Center for Epidemiologic Studies Depression Scale]

Depression Self-Rating Scale (Children's Version), 2465

Depression Symptom Inventory, 3809

Depressive Experiences Questionnaire, 2461

Depressive Experiences Questionnaire—Adolescent Version, 5511

Depressive Symptoms Measure, 5512

Depressive Symptoms Scale (French), 5513

Depth Scale, 4644

Derogatis Stress Profile, 3810

Description of Student Performance Aspects, 568

Descriptive Index, 1447, 1482

Design Recall Test, 2211

Desirability of Control Scale, 7072
Desirable Behavior Recognition Measure, 6228
Desire for Social Power Scale, 3129
Desire to Have Paid Employment Scale, 3130
Desire to Work Scale, 1995
Desired Job Characteristics Scale, 7376
Desperate Love Scale, 3995, 5746
Detention Locus of Control Scale, 4808
Developed Ability Performance, 6
Development Activities Benefits Scale, 6545
Development Opportunities Scale, 4645
Developmental Inventory of Feminine Values, 2302
Deviant Role/Identity Scale, 3202
Devotionalism Index, 3526
Diabetes Health Questionnaires, 4381
Diabetes Locus of Control Scale, 4809
Diabetes Quality of Life, 5514
Diagnostic Forced Choice Scale for First Line Supervisors, 1005
Diagnostic Inventory, 2375
Diagnostic Scale for Incest Survivors, 6407
Diagnostic Survey for Leadership Improvement, 2345
Dieting Beliefs Scale, 4810
Different Situations Inventory, 4812
Differential Emotions Scale, 5032, 5033
Differential Loneliness Scale, 2561, 5747
Differential Loneliness Scale (Finnish Version), 3996
Differential Personality Inventory, 845
Differentiation of Self Scale, 4811
Difficulty in America Scale, 1094
Diffuse Peer Group Index, 163

Diligence Inventory—Higher Education Form, 6634
Dimensions of Psychopathology in Middle Childhood, 412
Dimensions of Schooling, 1963
Dimensions of Self-Concept, 2056
Dimensions of Social Support Scale, 5748, 6260
Dimensions of Temperament Survey, 3356, 5034
Dimensions of Temperament Survey—Revised, 5035
Direct Comparison Test, 1154
Direct Coping Scale, 3811
Directiveness Scale, 3470, 3471
Disability Evaluation Scale, 4288
Disability Factor Scale, 6119
Disability Factor Scale G, 1780
Disabled Student Facilities Questionnaire, 1315
Disagreement over Children Scale, 4540
Disclosure Scale, 6340
Discomfort Anxiety Inventory, 5515
Discrimination Test, 1041
Discussion Topic Survey, 1295
Disordered Eating Test, 2833
Dispositional Stress Scales, 3812
Distress Scale, 2466
Distributional Rating Scale, 7298
Distributive Justice Evaluations Scale, 7221
Distributive Justice Index, 6546
Distributive Justice Scale, 234, 7222
Divergent Production of Semantic Classes Test, 110
Divergent Production of Semantic Transformations, 128
Divergent Production of Symbolic Implications Test, 129
Divergent Production of Symbolic Transformations, 111
Divergent Thinking Test, 608
Divorce Potential Index, 2976
Divorce Propensity Scale, 6408
Divorce Reaction Inventory, 2977

Dog and Bone Test, 1926
Dogmatism Scale, 926, 2259–2261, 5184, 7171 [See also Rokeach Dogmatism Scale; Trodahl and Powell Dogmatism Scale]
Dogmatism Scale, Form E, 1483
Dogmatism Scale, Short-Form, 2292, 7200 [See also Rokeach Dogmatism Scale—Short Form]
Doll Play and Maternal Interview Techniques, 927
Dominance-Accommodation Scale, 4382
Dominance Scale, 3472
Dot Estimation Task, 5036
Dove Test of Mental Aptitude, 72
Draw-a-Car Test, 846
Draw a Dog Scale, 1117
Dream Extraversion Scale, 5037
Dream Incident Technique, 30, 1655
Dream Questionnaire, 2737
Drews Parental Attitude Scale, 504
Drinking Expectancy Questionnaire, 4813
Drinking Inventory, 6229
Drinking Practices Questionnaire, 4383, 6230
Drinking Self-Efficacy Scale, 6231
Driving Anger Scale, 6232
Driving Motion Picture Test, 1384
Drug Abuse Attitude Scale, 505
Drug Attitude Questionnaire, 1155, 1781
Drug Attitude Scale, 1785
Drug Behavior Scale, 569
Drug Involvement Scale, 1214
Drug Issues Attitude Scale, 506
Drug Knowledge Scale, 343
Drug Knowledge Test, 344, 1042, 1600
Drug Knowledge, Use, and Attitude Questionnaire, 1858
Drug Number Scale, 1215
Drug Use Attitude Questionnaire, 507
Drug Use Questionnaire, 4384

Drug Use Survey, 6233
Drumcondra Verbal Reasoning Test, 887
DSM-III Bulimia Questionnaire, 4385
Dua Anxiety Expression Scale, 928
Dual-Career Family Scale, 6409 [See also Scales for Investigation of the Dual-Career Family—Revised]
Dual Employed Coping Scales, 6410
Dualism Scale, 3527
Duke Health Profile, 5516
Duncan Occupational Status Scale—Modified, 1470
Duncan Personality Integration Reputation Test (PIRT), 847
Duncan Residence Hall Counselor Evaluation Scale, 1006
Dunn-Lorge Figure Drawing Scale, 888
Duso Affectivity Assessment Device, 1964
Dutton Attitude Test, 508
Dyadic Adjustment Scale, 2978, 4541
Dyadic Adjustment Scale, Abbreviated, 2962
Dyadic Adjustment Scale—Revised, 4542
Dyadic Interaction Scale, 2911
Dyadic Parent-Child Interaction Coding System, 2979
Dyadic Relationship Scales, 3998
Dyadic System, 1251
Dyadic Trust Scale, 2562
Dying and Death Scale, 2467
Dymond Adjustment Index, Modified Version, 34
Dymond Rating Tests, 1385
Dysfunctional Attitude Scale, 4289, 5517
Dysfunctional Attitude Scale—Form A, 5518
Dysfunctional Attitude Survey, 6121

Dysfunctional Attitudes Scale, 4814, 6120
Dysfunctional Attitudes Scale—Form A, 3813, 4815

E

E Scale, 6744
Early Childhood Matching Familiar Figures Test, 2262
Early Elementary School Children Rating Scale, 1043
Early Mathematics Behaviors Tests, 345
Early Memories Test, 848
Early Resources Checklist, 5749
Early Retirement Questionnaire, 669
Early Trauma Checklist, 5519
EAS Temperament Survey, 5039, 7002
EASI-I Temperament Survey, 3357
EASI-III, 5038
EASI-III Test, 3358
East-West Questionnaire, 1782
Easterbrook and Goldberg Parent Attitude Scale, 6411
Eating Attitudes Test, 4290, 6234

Eating Attitudes Test-26, 6235
Eating, Drinking and Smoking Scales, 4386
Eating Related Characteristics Questionnaire, 4387
Echoic Response Inventory for Children, 7
Eclectic Protestant Ethic Scale, 3528
Economic Hardship Questionnaire, 4543
Economic Hardship Scale, 5520
Economic Strain Scale, 3814
Edmonds Marital Conventionalization Scale, 2980, 3019
Education Attitude Survey, 1783

Education Belief Scales, 4816
Education Scale VII, 2739
Educational Attitudes Inventory, 2738
Educational Attribution Scale, 3203
Educational Forces Inventory, 2057
Educational Goals Scale, 3068
Educational Innovation Attitude Scale, 1784
Educational Orientation Questionnaire, 3393
Educational Set Scale, 1068
Educational Vocational Counseling Survey, 670
Educational Work Components Study, 1341, 1786
Edwards Personal Preference Schedule, Poland's Modification of, 258 [See also EPPS ...]
Edwards Social Desirability Scale, 438, 3999
Effectance Test, 3069
Efficacy to Influence Change Scale, 3204
Effort versus Ability versus External Scale, 3205
Ego and Discomfort Anxiety Inventory, 5521
Ego Development Scale, 6372, 6373
Ego Development Test, 136
Ego Development Test (Short Version), 2948
Ego Identity Scale, 2949, 2950, 4497, 5040, 5041, 7003, 7004 [See also Rasmussen's Ego Identity Scale]
Ego Identity Status Measure, 628
Ego-Integrity Measure, 7005
Ego Involvement Scale, 3359
Ego Permissiveness Questionnaire, 3360
Ego Stage Development Inventory, 2951
Ego-Strength and Self-Esteem Measure, 3206
Ego Strength Scale, 2164
Ego Sufficiency Scale, 929

Eight Professors Scale, 866

Eisenman-Cherry Creativity Test, 609

Eisenman-Cherry Response Acquiescence Scale, 930

Elementary Grades Anthropology Achievement Tests, 1044

Elementary Guidance Workers' Effectiveness Questionnaire, 316

Elementary School Counseling Survey Form, 671

Elementary School Environment Survey, 1316

Elmore Psychological Anomie Scale, 413

Embedded Figures Motion Picture Test, 1386

Embedded Figures Test, 770

Emotion Assessment Scale, 5042

Emotional Adjustment Scale, 1656

Emotional Autonomy Scale, 4000, 4001, 4544, 6412

Emotional Autonomy Scale—Short Version, 7006

Emotional Closeness Scale, 4002

Emotional Control Questionnaire, 7007

Emotional Dependence Scale, 931

Emotional Empathy Scale, 3473 [See also Mehrabian and Epstein Emotional Empathy Scale]

Emotional Expressiveness Questionnaire, 7008

Emotional Intensity Scales, 7009

Emotional Maturity Scale, 2952

Emotional Self-Disclosure Scale, 6341

Emotional Stress Scale, 5522

Emotionality Scale, 7010

Emotions Profile Index, 2165

Empathic Concern Scale, 7172

Empathic Response Instrument, 3474

Empathy Scale, 235, 1387, 7173, 7174

Empathy Scale (Chapman), 771

Empathy Scale, Revised, 3506

Empathy Test, 3476

Employee Attitude Scale, 6122

Employee Attitude Survey, 1156, 2622

Employee Commitment Questionnaire, 1996

Employee Performance Evaluation by Supervisor Form, 1007

Employee Performance Self-Evaluation, 1008

Employee Rating Scale, 5277

Employee Reactions Measure, 6547

Employee Satisfaction Questionnaire, 164

Employee Stock Ownership Plans Satisfaction Measure, 4126

Employees' Expectancy Scale, 2362

Employment Characteristics Scale, 7011

Employment Commitment Scale, 3626

Employment Immobility Questionnaire, 3627

Employment Importance Scale, 3628

Employment Interview Rating Scales, 3574

Employment Satisfaction Questionnaire, 1577

Endemic Imagery Questionnaire, 3394

Energy Depletion Index, 4127, 5919

Engineering Interest Inventory, 3629

Engineering Interest Scale, 7377

Enjoyment of Mathematics Scale, 2740, 7073

Enriching and Nurturing Relationships, Issues, Communication and Happiness Questions: Alternate Version, 6413

Enrichment and Resource Depletion from Nonwork Scales, 5750

Environmental Assessment Index, 4545

Environmental Assessment Index—Short Form, 4546

Environmental Assessment Technique, 165, 672
Environmental Assessment Technique, Revised, 184
Environmental/Biological Attribution Scale, 6743
Environmental Checklist, 3070
Environmental Control Scale, 1997
Environmental Force Unit (EFU) Observational System, 1095
Environmental Forces Schedule, 673
Environmental Interferences Index, 6548
Environmental Robustness Scale, 4646
Environmental Satisfaction Inventory, 4647
Environmental Satisfaction Scale, 1965
Environmental Stress Scale, 3071
Environmental Supplies-Respondent Preferences Fit Questionnaire, 6549
Environmental Support Scales, 6550
Environmental Uncertainty Scale, 3072
Environmentally Responsive Behavior Questionnaire, 6236
Envy Questionnaire, 439
Episodic Long-Term Memory Questionnaire, 1601
Epistemological Belief Questionnaire, 6361
EPPS, Four Factor-Analytic Scales of, 216 [See also Edwards Personal Preference Schedule...]
Equal Opportunity Measure, 6551
Equity Sensitivity Instrument, 3395, 5751, 7223
Erikson Ego Epigenesis Test, 629
Erikson Psychosocial Stage Inventory—Revised, 4498 [See also Modified Erikson Psychosocial Stage Inventory]
Eriksonian Inventory, 2166

Eroticism Scale, 1157
Erwin Identity Scale, 5043, 6374
Estes Attitude Scale, 1787
Estes Reading Attitude Scale, 2741 [See also Reading Attitude Scale]
Estimate of Self-Competence Scale, 3207
Estimation Questionnaire, 4817
Ethical Behavior Rating Scale, 3529
Ethical Climate Questionnaire, 6552
Ethical Conflict Questionnaire, 3530
Ethical Reasoning Inventory, 2212, 3531
Ethical Risk Questionnaire, 971
Ethnic Acculturation Scale, 5752
Ethnic Identity Scale, 4818
Ethnic Identity Scales, 5753
Ethnic Stereotype Checklist, 4291
Evaluation Anxiety Scale, 3707
Evaluation of Behavioral Implications, 2564
Evaluation of Field Practice Supervision, 1317
Evaluation of School Functioning Index, 4388
Evaluation of Semantic Transformation Test, 267
Evaluation of Students Who Major in Social Work, 674
Evaluation of Symbolic Transformations Test, 112
Evaluation Rating Scale, 3575
Evaluation Sensitivity Scale, 283
Evans Reaction Inventory, 932 [See also Reaction Inventory]
Event Dimension Scales, 6553
Events Test, 772
Everyday Skills Competence Scale, 3672
Everyday Spatial Activities Test, 4389
Everyday Vision Questionnaire, 3815
Examinee Feedback Questionnaire, 6554

Exchange Approval Scale, 7299
Exchange Orientation Scale, 5754
Exchange Variables Scale, 7378
Executive Participation Scale, 2346
Exercise Identity Scale, 6745
Existential Anxiety Scale, 1657, 5523
Exner Self Focus Sentence Completion, 1484 [See also Self-Focus Sentence Completion]
Expectancy/Context Questionnaire, 6746
Expectancy Motivation, 4704
Expectancy Scale, 6747
Expectancy-Theory Scale, 6635
Expectation Survey, 719
Expectations about Counseling, 2058
Expectations about Counseling—B, 4819
Expectations about Counseling—Brief Form, 4821, 4822, 6748, 6749
Expectations about Counseling Questionnaire, 3208, 4820
Expectations about Counseling Questionnaire—Revised, 3210
Expectations about Counseling—Short Form, 3209
Expectations for College Scales, 6750
Expectations for Reemployment Scale, 6751
Expected Balance Scale, 3816
Expected Utility of Present Job Scale, 7379
Experience of College Questionnaire, 675
Experience Questionnaire, 5044
Experiences as a Mother Scale, 2981
Experiences Questionnaire, 130
Experimental Test of Testwiseness, 5127
Exploration Process Scale, 7380
Exploratory Study of Task Preferences, 205

Expressed Acceptance of Self, 4823
Expressed Emotion Questionnaire, 5045
Expressed Motivations Questionnaire, 720
Expression of Emotion Scale, 3361
Extended Objective Measure of Ego Identity Status, 5046, 6375, 7012
Extended Personal Attributes Questionnaire, 5047
Extent of Consideration Questionnaire, 7381
Extracurricular Involvement Inventory, 5409
Extraordinary Belief Inventory, 3211
Eyberg Child Behavior Inventory, 4390
Eysenck Impulsiveness Questionnaire, 6237

F

F-Scale, 2263, 2264 [See also Adorno F Scale; SF Test]
F Scale, Balanced (Short Form), 3460 [See also Short Balanced F Scale]
F Scale, Revised, 3507
FACES, 2982 [See also Family Adaptability and Cohesion ...]
FACES Scales—Revised, 2983
Facilitative Relationship Indicators Checklist, 7300
Faculty Attitudes about Unions Scale, 4292
Faculty Collegiality Scale, 5920
Faculty Competence Rating Scale, 1009
Faculty Evaluation Instrument, 1548
Faculty Orientations Study, 1788
Faculty Performance Checklist, 3576
Faculty Roles Rating Scale, 509

Faculty Stress Index, 5921
Faculty Support Scale, 6752
Faculty Trust in Colleagues Scale, 5922
Faculty Trust in the Principal Scale, 5923
Faculty Trust Scale, 5924
Fagerström Tolerance Question-naire, 6238
Fairness Perceptions Measures, 6555
Fairness Perceptions Scale, 6556
Faith in Management Scale, 5925
Faith Scale, 5226
Familiarization Matrix Test, 1467
Familism Scale, 4547
Family Adaptability and Cohesion Evaluation Scale III, 6415 [See also FACES]
Family Adaptability and Cohesion Evaluation Scales, 4550, 6414 [See also FACES]
Family Adaptability and Cohesion Scales (FACES II), 4549 [See also FACES]
Family Adaptation Scale, 4548
Family Affect Measure, 4551
Family Assessment Device, 4552
Family Authority Orientation Scale, 644
Family Behavior Checklist, 4553
Family Coping Inventory—Short Form, 2984
Family Crisis-Oriented Personal Scales, 6416
Family Environment Scale—Hebrew Short Form, 4554
Family Environment Schedule, 2985
Family Experiences Questionnaire, 6417
Family Expressiveness Question-naire, 6418
Family Expressiveness Question-naire—Self-Report Version, 6419
Family Functioning Scales, 6420

Family Functioning Style Scale, 6421
Family Interaction Questionnaire, 4499, 6422
Family Intrusion at Work Scale, 4555
Family Involvement Scale, 2986, 6423
Family Life Questionnaire, 6424
Family Living and Traditional Values Scales, 4556
Family Material Well-Being Scales, 2987
Family Needs Survey, 6425
Family of Origin Scale, 4824, 6426
Family-of-Origin Scale, Short Forms 1 and 2, 6427
Family Perception Grid, 4557
Family Proverbs Scale, 4558
Family Relation Inventory—Father, 645
Family Relations Inventory, 142, 1296
Family Resource Questionnaire, 2988
Family Ritual Questionnaire, 6428
Family Role Behavior Inventory, 4559
Family Sanctions Scale, 4560
Family Satisfaction Scale, 6429
Family Sense of Coherence Scale, 4561
Family Strength Scale, 4562
Family Stressor Scale, 6430
Family Structure Survey, 4563, 6431
Family System Test, 4564
Family Therapy Alliance Scale, 5278
Family Vignettes, 2989
Family→Work Conflict Scale, 6432
Family-Work Spillover Scale, 6433
FASTE, 3477
Fatalism Scale, 4825
Fear of AIDS Scale, 4293
Fear of Bodily Sensations Question-naire, 3817

Fear of Career Stagnation Scale, 4128
Fear of Commitment Scale, 3818
Fear of Consequence of Success Scale, 2410
Fear of Crime Scale, 3819
Fear of Death Scale, 1081, 2468, 2469, 3820 [See also Collett-Lester Fear of Death Scale]
Fear of Failure Scale, 3821
Fear of Intimacy Scale, 5755
Fear of Negative Evaluation, 3822
Fear of Negative Evaluation Scale, 3478, 5524
Fear of Negative Evaluation Scale—Brief Version, 5756
Fear of Powerlessness Scale, 5525
Fear of Success and Fear of Appearing Incompetent Scales, 2470
Fear of Success Questionnaire, 1658, 1659, 2411
Fear of Success Scale, 1660, 2412, 2471, 5526 [See also Zuckerman and Allison Fear of Success Scale]
Fear Questionnaire, 5527
Fear Questionnaire—Chinese Version, 7013
Fear Questionnaire Subscales, 3823
Fear Survey Schedule, 7014 [See also Modified Fear Survey]
Fear Survey Schedule for Children, 5528
Feedback Sheet, 3630
"Feeling Good" Booklet Test, 5374
Feelings and Concerns Survey, 5529
Feelings of Inadequacy Scale, 3212 [See also Janis-Field Feelings of Inadequacy Scale]
Feffer Role Taking Test, 1096 [See also Role-Taking Test]
Feldstein Affect Judgment Test, 1252
Felt Figure Replacement Technique, 440, 2167
FEM Scale, 1789, 7076

Female Faces Scale, 2363
Female Roles Questionnaire, 2742
Feminine Rating Scale, 284
Feminism Scale, 1790, 7074
Feminist-Antifeminist Belief-Pattern Scale, 1791
Feminist Identity Development Scale, 7075
Feminist Identity Scale, 4294, 6753
Fennema-Sherman Mathematics Attitude Scales, 6123
Fetal Health Locus of Control Scale, 4826
Field Interaction Scale, 1253
15 Personal Problems Inventory, 5279
Figural Intersections Test, 4226, 6124
Figural Memory Span Motion Picture Test, 1388
Figure Analogies Test, 2059
Figure Copying Test, 1734
Figure Ratings Task, 4827
Filial Expectancy Scale—Adapted, 2990
Filial Expectations Measure, 2991
Filial Piety Scale, 4565
Filial Responsibility Measure, 2992
Filial Responsibility Scale, 6434
Financial Concerns Scale, 3824
Financial Concerns Scale—Revised, 5530
Fireman Leadership Profiles, 1549
First Grade Adjustment Scale, 2413
First-Year Student Questionnaire, 5410
Fischer Pro-Con Attitude Scale, 2743
Fisher-Turner Attitudes toward Seeking Professional Psychological Help Scale, 6125 [See also Attitudes toward Seeking Professional Psychological Help Scale]
Fitzgibbons Patients' Self Perceived Treatment Need Scale, 773

Five Dimensional Religiosity Scale, 5227

Five Scales of Attitude, 83

Five Scales of Social Stratification in Czechoslovakia, 268

Flags, 3673

Flanders' Interaction Analysis System Achievement Test, Knowledge of, 1049 [See also Interaction Analysis System]

Flavell Spatial Egocentrism Scale, 1485

Florida Key of Learner Self-Concept—Revised, 3213

Florida Key Test, 1389

Florida Scale of Civic Beliefs, 972

Focus Scale, 7382

Focusing Inventory—State, 6239

Focusing Test, 1859

Folding Blocks Test, 2060

Follow-Up on Counseling Suggestions Questionnaire, 1010

Follow-Up Questionnaire on Individual Counseling, 4648

Food Preference Survey, 3396

Forced-Choice Guilt Inventory, 5048

Forced Vowel Selection Test, 1045

Ford Social Desirability Scale, 441

Foreign Language Attitude Scale, 2744

Foreign Policy Attitude Scale, 510

Foreman Job Responsibility Questionnaire, 1011

Foreman Survey Form, 1012

Form Identification Motion Picture Test, 1390

Formal Operational Reasoning Test, 3428

Formal Operations Assessment Battery, 3427

Formal Reasoning Tests, 889

Four Example-Anchored Descriptive Rating Scales, 215

Four Systems Anxiety Questionnaire, 3825

Four-Year to Two-Year College Student Transfer Questionnaire, 511

Fourth Grade Reading Preference Questionnaire, 1455

Framingham Scale, 5185

Framingham Type A Scale, 3479, 7175

Free Speech Questionnaire, 973

Free-Time Activities, 570

Free Will-Determinism Scale, 3532

Frequency of Disagreements Conflict Resolution Scales, 4003

Frequency of Discussion Checklist, 1297

Freshman Camps Expectation and Experiences Questionnaire, 774

Freshman Transition Questionnaire, 3709

Freshmen Experience Survey, 3708

Friedman School Principal Burnout Scale, 5926

Friedmans' Scale, 3533

Friendliness Questionnaire, 2565

Friendship Analysis Scale, 1097

Friendship Intimacy Questionnaire, 4004

Frustration, Emotional Reaction and Hostility Scales, 4129

Frustration Index, 5927

Frustration Measure, 1216

Frustration Scale, 2623, 4130

Frustration Scales, 2472

Frustration Strain Scale, 5531

Fuller Affective Interaction Records (FAIR), 1217

Functional Behavior Survey, 2834

Functionally Remote Associates Test (FRAT), 610

Fundamental Interpersonal Relations Orientation Behavior, 50

Fundamental Interpersonal Relations Orientation-Behavior Questionnaire, 5757

Fundamental Interpersonal Relations Orientation-Behavior Scale, 6240
Fundamental Interpersonal Relations Orientation Test, 51 [See also Schutz' Fundamental Interpersonal Orientations Test, Form B]
Fundamental Reading Competencies Test, 1602
Future Orientation Scale, 207
Future Time Orientation Scale, 7224
Future Time Perspective Inventory, 775

G

Gable-Roberts Attitudes toward School Subjects, 2745
Gambling Motivation Scale, 6636
Gambrill-Richey Assertion Inventory, 7176 [See also Assertion Inventory]
Games Inventory Scales, 1218
Garage Pride Scale, 5928
Gardner-Thompson Reference Valence Test, 974
Gay Stereotype Scale, 6754
Geer's Specific Fear Rating Sheet, 414
Gender Behavior Inventory for Boys, 1219, 1285
Gender Identity Interview Schedule, 7077
Gender Identity Procedure, 630
Gender Orientation Scale, 7078
Gender Power Scales, 3214
Gender Role Attitudes Scale, 6126
Gender Role Conflict Scale, 7079
Gender Role Conflict Scale-I, 5082
Gender Role Orientation, 2746
Gender Role Preferences Scale, 5084
Gender Role Scale, 5083

Gender Role Scales, 6127
General Alienation Scale, 442, 5758
General Anxiety Questionnaire, 933
General Anxiety Scale, 2473
General Attitude toward Business Scales, 84
General Attitude toward Institutional Authority Scale (GAIAS), 2747, 4295
General Behavioral Procrastination Scale, 6241
General Causality Orientations Scale, 4391
General Community Satisfaction Scale, 4649
General Decision-Making Style, 7124
General Health Questionnaire, 3826
General Health Survey, 5532
General High Altitude Questionnaire (GHAQ), 571
General Intolerance Scale, 1792
General Job Satisfaction Scale, 5929–5932
General Leadership Impression Scale, 6242
General Mental Health Questionnaire, 3830
General Modernity Scale, 301
General Opinion Survey, 4005
General Physical Health Symptoms Inventory, 3831
General Population Assertiveness Contingency Schedule, 3480
General Psychology Competency Examination, 5375
General Self-Efficacy Scale, 4829, 6756, 6757
General Self-Efficacy Scale— Revised, 6758
General Self-Esteem Scale, 2061
General Social Alienation Scale, 1098
General Statements Questionnaire, 4830, 4831
General Trust Scale, 5049

General Union Attitudes Scale, 6128

General Well-Being Questionnaire, 5533

General Well-Being Scale, 2474

Generalized Anxiety Questionnaire, 3827

Generalized Contentment Scale, 3828

Generalized Expectancy for Negative Mood Regulation, 3829

Generalized Expectancy for Success Scale, 4828

Generalized Expectancy of Sport Success Scale, 3215

Generalized Self-Efficacy Scale, 3216

Generalized Self-Efficacy Scale— Short Form, 6755

Generativity Scale, 6376

Gerard Rod and Frame Test, 776 [See also Rod and Frame Test]

Geriatric Depression Scale, 2475, 3832, 5534

Geriatric Evaluation by Relatives Rating Instrument, 2566

Geriatric Hopelessness Scale, 2476, 5535

Geriatric Interpersonal Evaluation Scale, 2213

Gesell School Readiness Tests, 469

Ghiselli Self-Description Inventory, 2265, 3131 [See also Self-Description Inventory]

Gibson Scribbles Test, 1391

Gilliland-Burke Measure of Social Intelligence, 1099

Glenn-Villemez Index of Productivity, 676

Gleser-Ihilevich Defense Mechanism Inventory, 850 [See also Defense Mechanism Inventory]

Global Assessment Scale, 3833, 5536

Global Dimension Appraisal Form, 3577

Global Hopelessness Scale, 3834

Global Job Classification Scale, 3073

Global Job Satisfaction Questionnaire, 4131

Global Job Skill Assessment, 5128

Global Parenting Authority Scale, 6435

Global Rating Blank, 317

Global Self Attitude Scale, 1793

Global Self-Worth Scale, 6759

Global Sexual Interest Scale, 4006

GM Faces Scale, 1578

Goal Assessment Scale, 4705

Goal Commitment Measure, 4706

Goal Commitment Scale, 6637, 6638

Goal Dimension Questionnaire, 4707

Goal Directedness Scale, 4708

Goal Instability Scale, 4132, 4500, 4709, 6639

Goal Instability Scale—Modified, 3835

Goal Orientation Scale—Classroom, 6761

Goal Orientation Scale—Sport, 6640

Goals and Strategies for Studying Science Questionnaire, 4832

Goals Inventory, 6641

Goldberg Articles Test, 975

Goldfarb Fear of Fat Scale, 2477

Good and Good Fear of Success Scale, 2478

Good and Good Social Power Motivation Scale, 3132

Gordon Test of Visual Imagery Control, 777, 6969

Gottheil's Oral Trait Scale, 934

Gough and di Palma Attitude Measure, 512

Gough-Sanford Rigidity Scale, 1486

Gould Manifest Alienation Measure, 443 [See also Manifest Alienation Measure]

Grade Contract Attitude Scale, 513

Grades and Grading Practices Questionnaire, 166

Graduate Environmental Perception Scales, 2062

Graduate Satisfaction Scale, 6557

Graduate Stress Inventory—Revised, 5411

Greenwood's Positive Social Behavior Scale, 2567

Gribbons-Lohnes Readiness for Vocational Planning, 470 [See also Readiness for Vocational Planning, Revised Edition]

Gross Cohesion Scale, 1710

Gross Rating of Facilitative Interpersonal Functioning Scale, 1889

Gross Ratings of Facilitative Interpersonal Functioning Scale, 1890

Grossman Interpersonal Sensitivity Measure, 444

Group Arousal Measure, 1998

Group Atmosphere Scale, 2568, 3074

Group Behavior Rating Scale, 778

Group Climate Questionnaire, 4650

Group Climate Questionnaire—Short Form, 5759

Group Cohesion, 4007

Group Cohesion Measure, 1711

Group Cohesiveness Index, 2569

Group Cohesiveness Scale, 1712, 4008

Group Conformity Measure, 445

Group Decision-Making Scale, 2912

Group Evaluation Form, 4651

Group Identification Scale, 4009

Group Importance Inventory, 4010

Group Incidents Questionnaire, 1860

Group-Interaction Measure, 5760

Group Inventory for Finding Creative Talent, 1927

Group Judgment Scale, 1392

Group Oral Performance Test, 1013

Group Participation Rating Scale, 53

Group Task Strategy Scale, 6342

Group Therapist Orientation Scale, 1254

Group Therapy Survey, 4833, 6129

Group Toy Preference Test, 2181

Growth Need Strength Measure, 4133

Growth Need Strength Measures, 1999

Gruen-Korte-Stephens Internal-External Scale, 1393

Gruen Traditional American Ideology Scale, 1158

Guess Who, 1713

Guidance Administrator Questionnaire, 677

Guidance Directors' and Supervisors' Questionnaire, 318

Guidance Needs Questionnaire, 31

Guidance Tests and Counseling Attitude Scale, 85

Guidelines for Analysis of Early Childhood Education Programs, 678

Guilt Inventory, 7177

Gulf War Attitude Scales, 6130

Guy Emotive Imaging Scale, 2063

H

H-Scale of Directiveness, 936

H-Scale of Warmth, 937

Haiman Open-Mindedness Scale, 935

Hair-Loss Concern Scale, 3836

Haller Occupational Aspiration Scale, 269, 897 [See also Occupational Aspiration Scale]

Halo Scale, 1891

Hamilton Anxiety Scale, 5187

Hamilton Psychiatric Rating Scale for Depression, 2479, 3837

Hamilton Rating Scale for Depression, 3838

Handedness Questionnaire, 7080, 7081
Handicap-Related Problems for Parents Inventory, 4566
Hands, 3674
Handwriting Legibility, 2376
Happiness and Optimism of General Outlook Questionnaire, 3839
Happiness Measures, 5537
Happiness Scale, 1661
Haptic Matching Task, 2266
Haptic Visual Matching Test, 285
Hardiness Scale, 4710, 5050
Hardy Divorce Scale, 4296
Hare Self-Esteem Scale, 2064
Harren Vocational Decision Checklist, 1579
Harris' Scale for Social Responsibility in Children, Mischel's Adaptation of, 58
Harter's Intrinsic/Extrinsic Orientation Scale, 7082
Harvey's "This I Believe" Test, 346
Hassles and Uplifts Scale, 5538
Hassles Scale, 3075, 3710, 5539
Hassles Scale for Children, 5540
Hawaiian Acculturation Scale, 5761
Hawaiian Middle Adolescent Personality Scale, 7015
Hayes Early Identification Listening Response Test, 1735
Hazard Perception Test, 2065
Health and Daily Living Form, 2835
Health and Daily Living Form— Revised Version, 5541
Health Behavior Checklist, 6243
Health Belief Model Questionnaire, 4836
Health Belief Scale, 4837
Health Complaints Scale, 5542, 5543
Health Concerns Questionnaire, 5544
Health Condition Scale, 5545

Health-Engenderingness Scale, 1487
Health/Fitness Status, 5546
Health Habits Scale, 1220
Health Interference Scale, 3840
Health Locus of Control Scale, 2066, 3217, 3218, 6763 [See also Wallston Health Locus of Control Scale]
Health Opinion Survey, 2067, 2480, 5085, 5547
Health Perception, 779
Health Perception Questionnaire, 6764
Health Professions Stress Inventory, 4134, 5933
Health-Promoting Lifestyle Profile, 5548
Health Resources Inventory, 2414
Health Survey, 4392
Health Worry Scale, 3841
Heart Disease Locus of Control Scale, 3219
Hebrew Visual Discrimination Test, 2377
Heilbrun Parent-Child Interaction Rating Scales, 646 [See also Parent-Child Interaction Rating Scales—Modified]
Help-Seeking Attitude Scale, 7225
Helpfulness of Assertive Interview Behaviors, 4834
Helping Attitudes Instrument, 6131
Helping Beliefs Inventory, 3578
Helping Dispositions Scales, 2267
Helping Efficacy Scale, 4835
Henderson Environmental Learning Process Scale, 3076
Henderson Environmental Learning Process Scale—Modified, 2993
Hereford Parent Attitude Survey, 6436 [See also Parent Attitude Survey (PAS)]
Hermans' Need Achievement Test, 721

Herrenkohl Feelings about Success and Failure Scale, 722
Herrmann Brain Dominance Profile, 5129
Heterosexual Attitudes toward Homosexuality Scale, 2748
Heterosexual Behavior Hierarchy—Female Form, 3842
Heterosocial Assessment Inventory for Women, 2570
Hierarchical Influence Index, 1892, 2236
Hieronymus Scale Values, 270
High School Personality Questionnaire, 851
High School Social Readjustment Scale, 2481
High School Study Habits Scale, 7125
Higher Education Opportunities Questionnaire, 167
Higher Learning Test, 347
Higher Order and Memory Level Test, 8
Higher Order Need Strength Instrument, 2000
Higher Order Need Strength Questionnaire, 2182
Highway Patrol Performance Assessment Form, 3579
Hipple Interpersonal Relationship Scale, 780
Hirees Adjectival Characterizations Scales, 7301
Hiring Expectations Measure, 6558
Hispanics in Business Scale, 6132
HIV Disease Knowledge Questionnaire, 5376
HIV Prevention Scale—Short Version, 6244
HIV Symptoms Scale, 5549
Hockey Competence Scale, 6765
Hogan Empathy Scale, 781, 1100, 2268, 7178
Hogan-Greenberger Adjective Checklist, 723
Holbrook-Oseretsky Scale, 348

Holistic Living Inventory, 2836
Holland Vocational Preference Inventory, 194, 195
Hollingshead Occupational Scale, 898
Hollingshead's Two Factor Index, 1471
Holt Intimacy Development Inventory, 2837
Home-Career Conflict Measure, 6437
Home Economics Attitudes Scale, 3631
Home Economics Behavioral Change Questionnaire, 572
Home Educational Environment Index, 2994
Home Educational Environment Interview Schedule, 1946
Home Environmental Forces Schedule, 1298
Home Environmental Measures, 1947
Home Index, 1472, 3444
Home Index Scale, 1473
Home Interview Schedule, 647
Home Leaving Cognition Scale, 6438
Home Observation for Measurement of the Environment, 1948, 2997, 2998, 4567
Homemakers Satisfaction Questionnaire, 2995
Homemaking Commitment Scale, 2996
Homework Style and Behavior Scale, 6245
Homophobia Scale, 3843, 4297, 6133
Homophobic Scale, 514
Homosexism Scale, 2749
Homosexism Scale—Short Form, 2750
Homosexual Attitudes Indicator, 6134
Homosexual Employment Belief Scale, 4838

Hood Religious Experience Episodes Measure, 1514 [See also Religious Experience Episodes Measure]
Hope Index, 3844
Hope Scale, 5552, 5553
Hopelessness Scale, 1662, 2483, 3845, 3846, 5550 [See also Beck Hopelessness Scale]
Hopelessness Scale for Children, 2482, 3847, 5551
Hopkins Symptom Checklist, 1663, 3848, 5555
Hopkins Symptom Checklist-25, Hmong Version, 5554
Hoppock Job Satisfaction Blank, 4135 [See also Job Satisfaction Blank]
Hoppock Job Satisfaction Blank— Short Form, 2624
Hoppock Job Satisfaction Scale, 5934 [See also Job Satisfaction Scale]
Hospice Attitude Scale, 4298
Hospital Behavior Rating Scale, 1861
Hospital Projective Test, 1488
Hospital Satisfaction Scale, 6559
Hostile Press Motivation Instrument, 1342
Hostility Inventory, 5188 [See also Buss Durkee Hostility Inventory]
Hostility Scale, 7016
Hostility Scales, 3850
Hostility Strain Scale, 7017
Hostility toward Women Scale, 7018
Household Coping Mechanism Scale, 6439
Housing Issues Questionnaire, 319
Housing Needs and Preferences Questionnaire, 867
Houston Stress Scale [See (University of) Houston Stress Scale]
How Career Groups Work Scale, 6766

How Do You Think—Form B, 1928
How Do You Think?, Form E, 6367
How Do You Think Inventory, 2168
How Groups Work Scale, 5762
How I Feel about Myself Inventory, 1394
How I See Myself Scale, 1395
Hoyt-Grim Pupil Reaction Inventory, 2347
Human Figure Drawing Projective Test, 32
Human Resources Practices Survey, 3077
Human Rights Questionnaire, 6136
Humanistic Work Belief, 7226
Humanitarian Scale, 6135
Humor Observation System, 4393
Humor Perceptiveness Test, 2680
Humor Perceptiveness Test— Revised, 2378
Humor Test, 1456
Hunt Test of Conceptual Structure, 604
Hurlbert Index of Sexual Desire, 6642
Husband Social Support Scale, 4568
Husband Support Scale, 6441
Husband's Emotion Work Scale, 6440
Hygiene and Grooming Test, 1603
Hypercompetitive Attitude Scale, 4711, 6137
Hypermasculinity Inventory, 4299
Hypothetical Role-Playing Test, 3481
Hypothetical Situation Questionnaire, 1101

I

I Feel-Me Feel Inventory, 2069
I, P, & C Scale, 4855 [See also Internal, Powerful Others, and Chance Scales; Levenson Internal, Powerful Others, and Chance Scales]

I Scale, 515
Icelandic Parent Development
    Inventory, 6377
IDEA Form H, 5280
Idea Inventory, 2931, 4839, 6767
Ideal Pupil Checklist, 1929
Ideal Teacher Checklist, 5281
Ideal Teacher Q-Sort, 679
Ideal Therapeutic Relationship
    Scale, 5282
Ideas of Reference Scale, 236
Identical Forms Test, 1604
Identification Scale, 143
Identification with a Psychological
    Group Scale, 5763
Identification with Orderliness
    Scale, 6560
Identity Achievement Scale, 1286,
    4501
Identity Achievement Status Scale,
    271
Identity Diffusion Scale, 6768
Identity Status Incomplete Sen-
    tences Blank for Women, 2237
Identity Status Questionnaire, 2238
Identity Style Inventory, 6769
Ideological Scale, 3534
I-E Locus of Control Scale, 3225,
    4847 [See also Internal-External
    Locus of Control Scale; Rotter I-E
    Scale]
I-E Scale, 1396, 2068, 3224 [See
    also Internal-External Scale;
    Rotter I-E Scale]
IJR Behavior Checklist for Parents,
    Teachers, and Clinicians, 2838
Illinois Course Evaluation Ques-
    tionnaire, 168
Illness and Sick-Role Scales, 3851
Illness Behavior Inventory, 2839,
    3220
Illness Effects Questionnaire, 5556
Image of Science and Scientists
    Scale, 1794
Imagery Difference Questionnaire,
    3397
Imaginal Processes Inventory, 7019

Imaginary Audience Scale, 5189
Imaginary Companion Question-
    naire, 1397
Imaginative Reactions to Pictures
    Test of Attitude toward Reading,
    516
Imitation and Comprehension
    English Test, 1046
Imitation and Comprehension Test,
    349
Impact of Event Scale, 2484, 3852,
    5557
Impact on Family Scale, Modified,
    6466
Impersonal Future Extension Scale,
    782
Impersonal Past Extension Test,
    783
Importance of Parenting Scale,
    4569
Importance Questionnaire, 1318
Importance to Identity Scale, 5764
Important Events Questionnaire,
    7302
Imposter Phenomenon Scale, 6770
Impression Management Scale,
    Revised, 6246
Impressions of Counselor Charac-
    teristics Scale, 4840
Impressions of University Setting
    Questionnaire, 680
Impulsiveness Scale, 3482, 7020
    [See also Barrett Impulsiveness
    Scale]
Impulsivity and Sensation Seeking
    Scales, 6643 [See also Sensation
    Seeking Scale]
Inappropriate Job-Related Behavior
    Rating Scale, 4394
Incest Attitudes Survey, 6138
Incest Blame Scale, 6442 [See also
    Jackson Incest Blame Scale]
Incest Experiences Questionnaire,
    4841
Incurable Disease Social Distance
    Scale, 4011

Independence Need Questionnaire, 1343

Independence of Work Habits Test, 1047

Index of Achievement Values, 2999

Index of Adjustment and Values, 1398, 3535, 4842 [See also Bills Index of Adjustment and Values]

Index of Adult Adjustment, 3854

Index of Communication, 99

Index of Depression, 1664

Index of Discrimination, 76

Index of Empathy, 5051

Index of Empathy for Children and Adolescents, 3483

Index of Evaluated Inequality, 3445

Index of Homophobia, 3855

Index of Interviewer Credibility, 7303

Index of Job Desirability, 4136

Index of Job Satisfaction, 2625

Index of Life Stress, 5558

Index of Novelty Seeking, 3133

Index of Organizational Reactions, 4137, 4138

Index of Perceived Inequality, 3446

Index of Performance Evaluation, 3580

Index of Personal Reactions, 4712

Index of Potential Suicide—Clinical Scale, 2485

Index of Responding, 1714

Index of Sex Role Orientation, 5086, 7087

Index of Social Position, Revised, 1474

Index of Spouse Abuse, 3000

Indicators of Quality, 681

Indik Work Motivation Scales, 1344

Individual Beliefs about Organizational Ethics Scale, 7227

Individual Differences Questionnaire, 3675, 5130, 7126

Individual Differences Questionnaire, Revised, 3440

Individual Imagery Test, 784

Individual Reading Readiness Inventory, 4227

Individual Sense of Competence Test, 2070

Individual Student Affective Performance Measure, 5412

Individual Study Practices Questionnaire, 169

Individual Tradition-Modernity Scale—Revised, 3536

Individualism-Collectivism Scale, 4012, 5765

Individualism-Collectivism Scale—Short Form, 7228

Individualism Scale, 7229

Individualism-Social Determinism Scale, 2571

Individualized Classroom Environment Questionnaire, 3078

INDSALES Measure, 4139

Industrial Relations Climate Scale, 4652

Ineffective Arguing Inventory, 6443

Infant Attribution Scale, 4570

Infant Behavior Questionnaire, 2840, 3362, 3676, 5052

Infant Characteristics Questionnaire, 1940, 3363, 6247

Infant Development Questionnaire, 4502

Infant Psychological Development Scale, 631, 1287

Infant Temperament Questionnaire, 3364, 3365, 5053

Infant Temperament Questionnaire, Revised, 3375 [See also Revised Infant Temperament Questionnaire]

Inferential Reading Comprehension Test, 1605

Inferred College Teacher Perceptions of Personal Adequacy Classroom Observation Scale, 785

Influence Behavior Questionnaire, 6248

Influence on Parents Scale, 3001

Influence Scale, 2626
Informal Reading Inventory, 350
Information Exchange, 4481
Information Hunt, 1606
Information-Privacy Values, Beliefs, and Attitudes Interview Schedule, 2751
Information Seeking Interest Measure, 868
Ingratiation Tactics Scale, 2841
Ingratiatory Behavior Scale, 6249
Initial Self-Efficacy Scale, 6771
Inner Speech about Self Scale, 6250
Innovation Strategy Scale, 4653
Innovativeness Scale, 3484, 4713, 7083
Inpatient Behavioral Rating Scale, 1862
Inservice Education Programs Evaluation Instruments, 1319
Institutional Functioning Inventory, 170
Institutional/Goal Commitment, 3398
Institutional Information Questionnaire, 171
Institutional Procedures in Colleges and Universities, 682
Instructional Materials Motivation Scale, 6644
Instructional Objectives Exchange Self-Appraisal Inventory, 3221
Instructional Preferences Inventory, 5087
Instructor Cognitive Operation Index, 1255
Instructor Evaluation Form, 2348
Instructor Evaluation Questionnaire, 1014
Instructor Evaluation Scale, 1550
Instructor Rating Form, 3581
Instructor Rating Scale, 2349
Instructor's Rating Scale, 320
Instrument for the Observation of Teaching Activities—Interview Scales, 1015

Instrument of Altruistic Motivation, 3134
Instrumental and Expressive Behavior Inventory, 4396
Instrumental Competence Scale for Young Children, 3677
Instrumental Normative Values Scales, 7230
Integrative Complexity, 2214
Intellectual/Academic Development Scale, 2953
Intellectual Achievement Responsibility Questionnaire, 786, 2071, 4843, 4845, 6772
Intellectual Achievement Responsibility Questionnaire—Revised, 4844
Intellectual Achievement Responsibility Scale, 3222, 3856
Intellectual Achievement Responsibility Scale/Modified, 2072
Intellectual Achievement Responsibility Scale, Revision of, 16
Intellectual and Personal Development, 2954
Intellectual Self-Confidence Scale, 2073
Intellectualism-Pragmatism Scale, 86, 1515
Intelligent and Unintelligent Behavior Scale, 4397
Intended Systematic Exploration Scale, 7383
Intense Ambivalence Scale, 2486
Intensity of Interorganizational [Relations] Scale, 1893
Intensity of Parental Punishment Scale, 1949
Intent to Engage in Assertive Interview Behavior, 4398
Intent to Leave Scale, 5935
Intent to Quit Scale, 5936
Intent to Quit the Profession Scale, 5938
Intent to Stay in Job Scale, 4140
Intent to Stay Scale, 5939
Intent to Turnover Scale, 5940

Intention to Quit the Organization Scale, 5937
Intention to Search Scale, 7384
Intention to Support Union Scale, 3399
Intention to Turnover Scale, 4141
Intentions to Seek Counseling Inventory, 6645
Interaction Analysis System, 1894 [See also Flanders' Interaction Analysis System Achievement Test, Knowledge of]
Interaction Anxiousness Scale, 2572, 5766
Interaction Coding System, 2913
Interaction Involvement Scale, 6343
Interaction Scale, 102, 237
Interaction Strain Questionnaire, 3002
Interactional Problem-Solving Inventory, 4013, 6444
Interconcept Distance, 1908
Intercultural Values Inventory, 5228
Interest Questionnaire, 7385
Interest Self-Rating Inventory, 196
Interest Survey, 7084
Intergeneration Communication, 103
Intergenerational Fusion Scale, 4571
Intergenerational Individuation Scale, 6445
Internal Control Index, 3223, 4846, 6773
Internal Control Scale, 238
Internal Dialogue Measure, 4482
Internal-External Control Proverbs Test, 1399
Internal-External Correspondence Scale (Revised), 4848
Internal-External Locus of Control Scale, 2074, 6774 [See also I-E Locus of Control Scale; Rotter Internal-External Locus of Control Scale]

Internal-External Scale, 4849 [See also I-E Scale; Rotter Internal-External Scale]
Internal, Powerful Others, and Chance Scales, 4850, 6775 [See also I, P, & C Scale; Levenson Internal, Powerful Others, and Chance Scales]
Internal Rewards Scale, 4142
Internal Scanning Scale, 2932
Internal Work Motivation Scale, 2001, 6646
Internalized Shame Scale, 7021
International Travel Questionnaire, 7085
Internationalism Scale, 1795
Interns' Expectancy and Attitude Scales, 4851
Interparental Conflict Scale, 4572, 4574
Interparental Conflict Scales, 3003
Interparental Influence Scale, 4573
Interpersonal Adjective Scales— Revised, 4014, 5767
Interpersonal Aggression Scale, 1221
Interpersonal and Administrative Behavior Scale, 1863
Interpersonal Checklist, 787, 5768
Interpersonal Communication Competence Scale, 4483
Interpersonal Communication Satisfaction Inventory, 6344
Interpersonal Competency Scale, 446
Interpersonal Conflict Response Inventory, 2573
Interpersonal Conflict Scale, 1950, 4015, 5769, 6447
Interpersonal Control Scale, 2075
Interpersonal Dependency Inventory, 1715, 2574, 5770, 5771
Interpersonal Differentiation Test, 788
Interpersonal Facilitative Functioning Questionnaire, 1716
Interpersonal Facility Scale, 7179

Interpersonal Flexibility Scale, 217
Interpersonal Future Likelihood Inventory, 4852
Interpersonal Index, 447
Interpersonal Interaction Analysis, 448
Interpersonal Jealousy Scale, 2575, 3485
Interpersonal Jealousy Scale (Revised), 4016
Interpersonal Judgment Scale, 1717
Interpersonal Network Questionnaire, 4484
Interpersonal Orientation Scale, 54, 4017
Interpersonal Perception Method—Modified, 2076
Interpersonal Problem-Solving Assessment Technique, 2576
Interpersonal Rating Scale, 5772
Interpersonal Reactivity Index, 5773
Interpersonal Relations Scale, 2577, 5776
Interpersonal Relations Scale Checklist, 5777
Interpersonal Relations Scale Semantic Differential, 5778
Interpersonal Relationship Assessment Technique, 5774
Interpersonal Relationship Rating Scale, 1102, 1256
Interpersonal Relationship Scale, 5775 [See also Modified Interpersonal Relationship Scale]
Interpersonal Relationships Scale, 4018
Interpersonal Style Inventory, 1489 [See also Lorr Interpersonal Style Inventory]
Interpersonal Support Evaluation List, 2578, 5779–5781
Interpersonal Trust Scale, 1718, 2269, 2914, 4019, 5782 [See also Rotter Interpersonal Trust Scale]
Interpersonally Based Problem-Solving Scale (IBPS), 3429

Interpreting Data, 1607
Interracial Attitudes Questionnaire, 517
Interrole Conflict Scale, 6448
Intervention Rating Profile, 3400, 6139, 6561
Interview for Antisocial Behavior, 4399
Interview Rating Scale, 1864
Interview Reaction Questionnaire, 589
Interview Schedule for Predicting High School Grades, 471
Interviewer Perception Scale, 4853
Interviewer Trustworthiness Scale, 938
Interviewer's Postinterview Questionnaire, 5284
Interviewer's Preinterview Questionnaire, 5283
Intimacy and Eye Contact Scales, 1257
Intimacy Attitude Scale—Revised, 2579
Intimacy of Self-Disclosure Scale, 1895
Intimacy Scale, 2580, 3004, 6449
Intimate Relations Scale, 6450
Intolerance of Ambiguity Scale, 1796, 2077, 4854, 7180 [See also Ambiguity Tolerance Scale; AT-20; Revised Scale for Ambiguity Tolerance; Scale of Tolerance-Intolerance of Ambiguity; Tolerance for Ambiguity...]
Intolerance of Trait Inconsistency, 2078
Intragroup Conflict Scale, 5783
Intrinsic Job Characteristics Scale, 6562
Intrinsic Motivation Scale, 3136
Intrinsic Satisfaction Scale—Sport, 7086
Intrinsic Task Interest Scale, 3137
Intuitive Ability Test, 3430
Invasion of Privacy Questionnaire, 1320, 2079

Invasion of Privacy Scale, 2752
Invented Spelling Test, 7127
Inventory of Adolescent Attach-
    ments, 4020
Inventory of Anxiety in Decision
    Making, 2270
Inventory of Beliefs Related to
    Obsession Scale, 5559
Inventory of Career Attitudes, 2753
Inventory of College Activities, 172,
    683
Inventory of College Students'
    Recent Life Experiences, 5408
Inventory of Common Problems,
    3857
Inventory of Faculty Attitudes,
    1159
Inventory of Family Feelings, 1951
Inventory of Family Relationships,
    3005
Inventory of Female Values, 2303
Inventory of Home Stimulation,
    1952 [See also Caldwell Inven-
    tory of Home Stimulation]
Inventory of Interpersonal Prob-
    lems, 4021, 4022, 5784
Inventory of Learning Processes,
    3431, 4400, 5131, 5132, 7128
Inventory of Learning Processes—
    Short Form, 5133
Inventory of Parent and Peer
    Attachment, 6451
Inventory of Parent and Peer
    Attachment—Revised Scale,
    6452
Inventory of Personal Characteris-
    tics #7, 7022 [See also Personal
    Characteristics Inventory]
Inventory of Physical Symptoms,
    3858, 5560
Inventory of Psychosocial Balance,
    4503
Inventory of Psychosocial Develop-
    ment, 632, 1941, 2955
Inventory of Religious Activities
    and Interests, 1580
Inventory of Self-Appraisal, 472

Inventory of Socially Supportive
    Behaviors, 4023, 4401, 5785
Inventory of Teacher Characteris-
    tics, 684
Inventory of Teacher Social and
    Behavioral Standards, 3711
Inventory of Teacher-Student
    Relationships, 2416
Inventory of Teaching Factors, 1551
Inventory of Temporal Experiences,
    1400, 2080
Inventory of Test Anxiety, 1627
    [See also Test Anxiety Inventory]
Inventory to Diagnose Depression,
    3859, 5561
Investigatory Activities Inventory
    (Revised), 724
Iowa Pegboard Fine-Motor Task,
    4504
Iowa Picture Interpretation Test,
    1345, 1448
Iowa Self-Assessment Inventory,
    3853
Irrational Belief Measure, 4856
Irrational Beliefs Test (IBT), 1516,
    1665, 3226, 4857
Irrational Heterosocial Beliefs
    Scale, 4858
Irrational Personality Trait Inven-
    tory Scale—Revised, 3227
Irritation/Strain Scale, 2627
Islamic Work Ethic and Individual-
    ism Scales, 5229
Israeli Army Questionnaire for
    Personality and Motivation
    Measurement, 3582
Israeli Fear Survey Inventory, 1966
Issue Involvement Scale, 6140,
    7231
Issues Checklist, 6453
It Scale for Children, 137
Italian Stereotype Scale, 3228
Itching Scale, 5562
Item Distractor Efficacy Test, 173
It's Fun to Think, 2215

J

Jackson Incest Blame Scale, 6776
[See also Incest Blame Scale]
Jackson's Personality Research
Form, 218
Jaloweic Coping Scale, 3860
James I-E Scale, 1401, 2081
Janis-Field-Eagly Self-Esteem
Scale, 2082
Janis-Field Feelings of Inadequacy
Scale, 1402, 3229, 3861 [See also
Feelings of Inadequacy Scale]
Janis Field Feelings of Inadequacy
Scale—Revised, 6777
Japan Knowledge Test, 351
Jealous Responses Scale, 5786
Jealousy Coping Scale, 4402
Jealousy Scale, 3006
Jewish-American Identity Scale,
1403
Jiritsu Scale, 5787
Job Affect Scale, 3862, 4143, 5563
Job Alienation—Modified, 5941
Job and Organizational Attributes
Scale, 6563
Job and Work Avoidance Scale,
5942
Job and Work Satisfaction Scales,
5943
Job Associate-Bisociate Review
Index, 5285
Job Attitude Questionnaire, 1346
Job Attitude Survey, 2754
Job Attitudes Instrument, 4300
Job Attributes Questionnaire, 4654
Job Autonomy Questionnaire, 6564
Job Burnout Inventory, 2628
Job Career Key, 3678
Job Characteristics Inventory,
3080, 6565
Job Characteristics Scale, 6566
Job Choice Scale, 5324
Job Climate Questionnaire, 1967

Job Cognitions Scale—Adapted,
4144
Job Complexity Scale, 2083, 6567
Job Components Inventory, 3081
Job Components Inventory II, 3082
Job Conditions Questionnaire, 1404
Job Content Innovation Scale, 6568
Job Control Scale, 6569
Job Decision Style Questionnaire,
3632
Job Demand and Discretion Scales,
6570
Job Dependency Scales, 4145
Job Description Index, 1552, 1581
Job Description Scales, 6571
Job Descriptive Index, 1321, 2629
Job-Descriptive Index for Accoun-
tants, 4146
Job Descriptive Index—Modified,
2630
Job Descriptive Index—Shortened
Version, 5944
Job Desirability Exercise, 6647
Job Diagnostic Survey, 2631, 4859,
5945
Job Diagnostic Survey—Revised,
6572
Job Diagnostic Survey—Short
Version, 4147
Job Distress Scale, 5946
Job Experience Survey, 6251
Job Feedback Survey, 3083
Job Frustration Questionnaire,
5947
Job-Induced Anxiety Measure, 1666
Job Induced Tension Scale, 5948
Job Interests List, 197
Job Interference Scale, 5949
Job Interview Performance Expec-
tations Scale, 1736
Job Interview Performance Self-
Rating Scale, 2350
Job Investment Scale, 7386
Job Involvement and Psychological
Success Scales, 3583
Job-Involvement/Central-Life-
Interest Measure, 5325

Job Involvement Measure, 3635, 5326
Job Involvement Questionnaire, 1737, 2364, 2632
Job Involvement Questionnaire—Short Form, 5327
Job Involvement Scale, 2002, 2003, 3634, 3636, 3637, 4148, 5328, 5329, 5950, 7387–7390
Job Involvement Scale—Short Form, 1322, 5330, 7391
Job Involvement Semantic Differential, 3633
Job Involvement/Valued Self Measure, 5331
Job Knowledge Survey, 2380
Job Loss Perceptions Scale, 6778
Job Motivation Scales, 3138
Job Perception Scales, 2633
Job Performance Appraisal Checklist, 1016
Job Performance Constraints Scale, 4149
Job Performance Questionnaire, 1553
Job Performance Rating Form, 5286
Job Performance Rating Scale, 5287, 7304
Job Performance Scale, 4860, 7305
Job Performance Scales, 3584
Job Problems Scale, 1968
Job Reactions Survey, 4403
Job Recruiters' Evaluation of Military Experience Questionnaire, 518
Job Related Tension Index, 1667, 2638–2640
Job Rewards Scale, 5951
Job Satisfaction Blank, 4150 [See also Hoppock Job Satisfaction Blank]
Job Satisfaction Index, 1582
Job Satisfaction Inventory, 709
Job Satisfaction Measure, 1583, 2365, 2366, 4151, 4152 [See also Measure of Job Satisfaction]
Job Satisfaction Questionnaire, 1584, 1585, 2367, 4153, 5952, 5953
Job Satisfaction Scale, 1586, 2368, 2634–2637, 4154–4160, 5954–5968 [See also Hoppock Job Satisfaction Scale]
Job Satisfaction Scale—Modified, 5969
Job Scope Scale, 6573, 6574
Job Search Behavior Index, 7392
Job Search Scales, 5332
Job Skills Rating Scale, 5288
Job-Specific Index, 174
Job Stress Questionnaire, 2641, 4161
Job Stress Scale, 5970
Job Stress Scales, 2642
Job Stressors Interview, 6779
Job Structure Profile, 3084
Job Tedium Scale, 2643
Job Tension and Stress Scales, 5971
Job Tension Scale, 4162, 5972–5974
Job Time-Demands Scale, 2644
Job Treatment Index, 3085
Job Values Questionnaire, 321
Job Withdrawal Cognitions Scale, 7393
Job Withdrawal Intentions Scale, 5975
Jobs-Career Key, 2379, 3079
Johnson-Kenney Screening Readiness Test, 1118
Joiners' Scale, 5882
Jourard Level of Verbal Self Disclosure Scale, 590
Jourard Self-Disclosure Questionnaire, 591 [See also Self-Disclosure Questionnaire]
Jourard Tactile Body Accessibility Scale, 592
Jourard's Self-Disclosure Scale, 1258 [See also Self-Disclosure Scale]
Judging Criteria Instrument, 1930
Judgment Accuracy Test, 890
Judgment Analysis, 1457, 2183

Judgment of Line Orientation Test, 6053
Judgment Test, 9
Junior High School Desegregation Questionnaire, 1160
Junior Index of Motivation Scale, 2004
Juror Bias Scale, 7181
Just World Scale, 3537, 7232
Just World Scale—Chinese Version, 3538
Juvenile Delinquency Attitude Scale, 519

K

Kagan Cognitive Style Test, 939
Kammeyer's Role Choice Questionnaire, 869
Kansas Family Life Satisfaction Scale, 4575
Kansas Marital and Parental Satisfaction Scales, 6454
Kansas Marital Satisfaction Scale, 3007, 4576, 6455
Kansas Parental Satisfaction Scale, 3008
Kansas Reflection-Impulsivity Scale, 1490
Kassarjian I-O Social Preference Scale, 789
Kastan Questionnaire, 4793
Kastenbaum Future Density Test, 790
Katz & Braly Racial Stereotype Inventory, 520
Kaufman's Scale of Status Concern, 1475 [See also Status Concern Scale]
Kelly Role Construct Repertory Test, 219 [See also Role Construct Repertory Test]
Kelly's Role Construct Repertory Test, Bieri's Modification of, 47 [See also Bieri Grid; Role Construct Repertory Test—Grid Form]
Kennedy Institute Phonics Test, 1048
Kent Infant Development Scale (Modified), 4505
Kenyon Attitude toward Physical Activity Scale, 791 [See also Attitude toward Physical Activity Inventory]
Khatena-Morse Multitalent Perception Inventory, 4861
Kilmann Insight Test, 2304
Kindergarten Performance Profile, 2381
Kindergarten Reading Questionnaire, 352
Kindergarten Screening Battery, 6054
Kindness Picture-Story Measure, 113
Kinship Responsibility Index, 4577
Kinship Scale—Revised, 5788
Kirton Adaption-Innovation Inventory, 3432, 4024, 5134 [See also Adaptation-Innovation Inventory]
Knowledge of Behavioral Principles as Applied to Children, 2382, 3679
Knowledge of Depression Test, 5377
Knowledge of Development Scale, 5378
Knowledge of Infant Development Scale, 1050
Knowledge of Marijuana Test, 353
Known-Word Vocabulary Test, 354
Knudsen-Vaughn Index, 685
Kogan's Attitudes toward Old People Scale, 2755
Kohlberg Development Hierarchy of Private Speech Forms, 1491

Kohlberg's Moral Judgment Scale, 633 [See also Moral Judgment Scale]

Kohn Problem Checklist, 1082

Kolb-Boyatzis Feedback Analysis Form, 1259

Kuder Preference Record, Vocational Form C, Knowledge Test of, 10

L

LAM Scale, 5230

Language Attitude of Teachers Scale, 6141

Language Attitude Scale, 2756

Language Comprehension Test, 355

Larsen Aggression Scale, 940

Laterality Index, 2681

Lau-Ware Health Locus of Control Scale—Short Form, 4862

Law-Abidingness Scale, 287

Law and Order Test, 1797

Law-Related Attitudes Test, 1798

Lawrence Assertive Inventory, 2271

Lawrence-Lorsch Conflict Instrument, 1865

Leader Behavior Description Scale, 2843 [See also Leadership Behavior...]

Leader Behavior Rating Scale, 1866

Leader Hierarchical Influence Scale, 1554

Leader Leader-Member Exchange Measure, 6345

Leader-Member Exchange Measure, 1896

Leader-Member Exchange Scale, 4404, 4405, 6346

Leader-Member Exchange Scale—Member Form, 2916 [See also Member View of Leader-Member Exchange Scale]

Leader-Member Exchange Scale—Revised, 2915

Leader Power and Influence Scales, 6252

Leader Power Inventory, 6253

Leader Technical Competence Scale, 1555

Leadership Assessment Scales, 4406

Leadership Behavior and Description Questionnaire, 2084 [See also Leader Behavior ...]

[Leadership Behavior Description Questionnaire, Form XII], Initiating Structure Scale, 2842

Leadership Inventory, 2844

Leadership Measure, 6254

Leadership Opinion Questionnaire, 2682

Leadership Practices Inventory, 4407

Leadership Scale for Sports, 4408

Leadership Style Scale, 2845

Leadership Substitutes Scale, 4409

Learned Helplessness Questionnaire, 6255

Learning and Knowledge Attitudes Questionnaire, 521

Learning and Study Strategy Inventory, 5135

Learning Attitudes Scale, 6648

Learning Climate Inventory, 1323

Learning Context Questionnaire, 6362

Learning Environment Inventory, 473, 686, 1324

Learning Focus Inventory, 1867

Learning Instrument, 175

Learning Interdependence Scales, 5413

Learning Materials Questionnaire, 1325

Learning Orientation/Grade Orientation Scale, 2757, 5414 [See also LOGO...]

Learning Strategy Scale, 7129

Learning Structure Questionnaire, 1969

Learning Style Inventory, 2216, 5136
Learning Style Inventory—Korean Version, 7130
Learning Style Questionnaire, 5137
Learning Style Scale, 7131
Learning Tasks Scale, 1868
Least Preferred Co-Worker Questionnaire, 1458
Least Preferred Coworker Scale (LPC), 941, 2184, 3401, 4025, 5089
Least Preferred Co-Worker Scale—Revised, 5088
Leathers Credibility Scale, 6347
Lecture Evaluation Instrument, 3086
Lee-Lyon Self-Esteem Q-Sort, 792
Leisure Activities Questionnaire, 198, 870, 2185
Leisure Activities Rating Scales, 7088
Leisure Ethic Scale, 4301
Leisure-Income Tradeoff Scale, 5976
Leisure Satisfaction Measurement, 5564
Leisure Satisfaction Scale, 6780
Leisure Satisfaction Scale—Revised, 7089
Leisure Values and Preferences Scale, 6781
Leniency Scale, 4410, 7023
Lethal Behaviors Scale, 4411
Letter Discrimination Test, 1051
Letter Formation Test, 1052
Letter Identification Test, 1608
Letter-Like Forms Visual Discrimination Test, 356
Level of Care and Utilization Survey, 6575
Level of Expressed Emotion Scale, 7024
Level of Motivation for Retraining Scale, 3139
Levels of Emotional Awareness Scale, 5054

Levels of Learning Scales, 5138
Levenson Internal, Powerful Others, and Chance Scales, 1405 [See also Chance Scale; I, P, & C Scale; Internal, Powerful Others, and Chance Scales]
Levenson Locus of Control Questionnaire, 3230
Levenson Locus of Control Scale, 1406 [See also Locus of Control Scale; Locus of Control Scale—Brief Version]
Levy Optimism-Pessimism Scale, 2487
Lexington Attachment to Pets Scale, 5789
Liberalism-Conservatism Scale, 2305
Libertarian Democracy Scale, 1799
Library Attitude Scale, 2758
Library Research Strategies Questionnaire, 7132
Liebert-Morris Worry-Emotionality Scale, 5415 [See also Worry-Emotionality Scale; Worry-Emotionality Scale, Revised]
Life Activities Achievement Scale, 4714
Life Activities Inventory, 4026
Life Change Inventory, 1942
Life Changes Scale, 3009
Life Esteem Survey, 5231
Life Events Checklist, 2488, 5565
Life Events Questionnaire, 2581
Life Events Scale, 3863, 3864
Life Events Survey for Collegiate Athletics, 5566
Life Experience Scale, 1719
Life Experiences Survey, 2489, 3865–3867, 5567–5570
Life Experiences Survey—Modified, 3868
Life History Questionnaire, 1288
Life Optimism Test, 4863
Life Orientation Test, 5571–5574
Life Priorities, Q-Sort, 4027
Life Regard Index (Dutch), 3869

Life Role Importance and Involvement Scales, 6456
Life Role Salience Scales, 4578, 6142
Life Satisfaction Index—Form A, 5575
Life Satisfaction Index—Greek Version, 5576
Life Satisfaction Questionnaire, 5577
Life Satisfaction Rating Scale, 33
Life Satisfaction Scale, 415, 3870–3873, 5578–5581
Life Strain Scale, 6457
Life Style Orientation Questionnaire, 2186
Life Styles for Women, 1800
Life Success Measures Scale, 5582
Lifestyle Approaches Index, 6649
Lifestyle Exercise Inventory, 6256
Lifestyle Index, 3638
Lifetime Sexual Involvement Scale, 6257
Likert Organizational Profile, 1970
Likert Profile of a School Principal Questionnaire, 1407
Likert Profile of a School Teacher Questionnaire, 1408
Liking for Short Stories Scale, 7090
Liking for Subordinate Scale, 4028
Liking People Scale, 2582
Liking Scale, 55, 5090
Lincoln-Oseretsky Motor Development Scale, 634
Lindgren Embedded Figures Test, 3231
Link Together Test, 1931
Lipsitt Self-Concept Scale, 3232
List of Courses in Nursing, 3639
Listening Test, 2217
Literal Reading Comprehension Test, 1609
Litigaphobia Scale, 3874
Little Parental Valuing Styles Scale, 3010
Litwin and Stringer Organizational Questionnaire—Form B, 6782

Living Environment Scale, 3087
Local Union Structure Scale, 6576
Localism-Cosmopolitanism Scale, 2306
Locke Wallace Short Marital Adjustment Test, 3011 [See also Marital Adjustment Test; Short Marital Adjustment Test]
Locus of Conflict Rating Scale, 1628, 2085
Locus of Control Inventory, 6783
Locus of Control Inventory for Three Achievement Domains, 2086, 3233, 4865
Locus of Control Measure, 3234
Locus of Control of Interpersonal Relationships Questionnaire, 2087
Locus of Control Scale, 793, 2088–2090, 3235–3240, 4864, 4866–4870, 6784–6788 [See also Levenson Locus of Control Scale]
Locus of Control Scale, Adapted, 2091
Locus of Control Scale—Brief Version, 6789 [See also Brief Locus of Control Scale; Levenson Locus of Control Scale]
Locus of Control Scale for Children, 239, 2092, 3241 [See also Nowicki-Strickland Locus of Control Scale]
Locus of Control Scale for Children's Perceptions of Social Interactions, 3242
Locus of Control Scale—Modified, 4871
Locus of Control Test, 2093
Logic of Confidence Questionnaire, 4029, 7306
Logic of Confidence Scale, 4872
Logical Thinking Ability Test, 7133
LOGO: F, 6577
LOGO Scale, 3402 [See also Learning Orientation/Grade Orientation Scale]
LOGO II, 6650

London-Robinson Imagery Test, 794
Loneliness and Social Dissatisfaction Measure, 2583
Loneliness and Social Dissatisfaction Scale, 5790
Loneliness Inventory, 5791
Loneliness Questionnaire—Revised, 4030
Loneliness Rating Scale, 4031, 5792
Loneliness Scale, 5793
Long-Term Personal Direction Scale, 4873, 6651
Lorr Interpersonal Behavior Inventory, 1720
Lorr Interpersonal Style Inventory, 2169 [See also Interpersonal Style Inventory]
Loss of Face Scale, 5794
Loss Questionnaire, 5583
Louisville Behavior Checklist, 573
Louisville Fear Survey for Children, 2490
Louisville Fear Survey Schedule, 3875
Love Addiction Scale, 2584
Love/Hate Checklist, 4032 [See also Revised Love/Hate Checklist]
Love Relationship Scale, 4033
Lovesickness Scale, 3012
Low Back Self-Efficacy Scale, 6790
Low Self-Esteem Scale, 272
Lowenfeld Mosaic Test, 138
Loyalty Scale, 7394
Loyola Sentence Completion Blank for Clergymen, 1668
Lynn Achievement Motivation Questionnaire, 1347

M

MacDonald-Tseng Internal-External Locus of Control Scale, 2094
MacDonald's Poverty Scale, 522

Mach IV, 5190 [See also Machiavellianism Scale]
Mach IV, Gender-Free, 5186 [See also Machiavellianism Scale]
Mach IV Scale, 1492, 3486 [See also Machiavellianism Scale]
Mach V Scale, 3487, 7182 [See also Machiavellianism Scale]
Machiavellianism Scale, 1517, 1721 [See also Mach ...]
Macho Scale, 2759
Magazine Recognition Test, 5379
Magical Ideation Scale, 3539
Magnitude Estimation Scale for Human Values, 3540
Maine Scale of Paranoid and Nonparanoid Schizophrenia, 2491
Mainstreaming Attitude Inventory for Day Care Providers, 6143
Make a Picture Story, 56
Making Visual Discriminations Test—Modified, 357
Maladjustment Scale, 2492
Malaise Inventory, 5584
Male-Female Relations Test, 7091
Male Function Profile/Impotence Questionnaire, 6258
Male Influence on Female Career Choice Scale, 710
Male Role Quality Questionnaire, 7092
Male Sex-Role Attitude Survey, 2760
Male Social-Sexual Effectiveness Scale, 4034
Mammography Questionnaire, 6791
Management Behavior Questionnaire, 4412
Management Behavior Survey, 4413
Management-of-Difference Exercise, 5091
Manager Mentoring Scale, 4035
Managerial Attitudes Scale, 523
Managerial Competence Scale, 3243

Managerial Frames of Mind Survey—Revised, 7093
Managerial Performance Scale, 3585
Managerial Potential Scale, 3586
Managerial Support Scale, 4655
Managers Need Satisfaction Questionnaire, 1348
Manager's Role Questionnaire, 4874
Managing People Inventory, 3366
Managing Students Scale, 6792
Mandler-Cowan's Test Anxiety Questionnaire for High School Students—Short Form, 392 [See also Test Anxiety Questionnaire]
Mandler-Sarason Test Anxiety Questionnaire, 1629 [See also Sarason Test Anxiety Questionnaire; Test Anxiety Questionnaire]
Mandler-Sarason Test Anxiety Scale, 3712 [See also Sarason Test Anxiety Scale; Test Anxiety Scale]
Manifest Alienation Measure, 1103 [See also Gould Manifest Alienation Measure]
Manifest Anxiety Defensiveness Scale, 3488
Manifest Anxiety Scale, 3876, 5191, 5585 [See also Taylor Manifest Anxiety Scale]
Manifest Anxiety Scale, Children's Form, 29, 1493, 1647 [See also Children's Manifest ...; Revised Children's Manifest Anxiety Scale]
Manifest Needs Questionnaire, 2005, 4715–4717, 6653
Mann Test Anxiety Scale, 393
Marble in the Hole Game, 725
Margolis-Thomas Measure of Narcissism—Revised, 5192
Marijuana Frequency Scale, 1222
Marijuana Stage Scale, 1223
Marital Activities Inventory, 3013

Marital Adjustment Scale, 3014, 4579 [See also Marriage Adjustment Scale]
Marital Adjustment Test, 1299, 3015 [See also Locke Wallace Short Marital Adjustment Test]
Marital Alternative Scale, 3016
Marital Burnout Scale, 6458
Marital Communication Inventory, 3017, 6459
Marital Comparison Level Index, 3018
Marital Conflict Scale, 4580
Marital Consensus Scale, 6460
Marital Coping Inventory, 4581
Marital Disaffection and Disharmony Scales, 3020
Marital Goal-Orientation Scale, 3021
Marital Happiness Scale, 3022
Marital Influence Scale, 4582
Marital Instability Index, 3023
Marital Instability Scale, 6461
Marital Interaction Coding System, 3024
Marital Interaction Satisfaction Scale, 3025
Marital Quality Inventory, 6462
Marital Quality Scale, 3026
Marital Relationship Scale, 4583, 6464
Marital Relationships Equity Scale, 6463
Marital Satisfaction and Problem-Solving Scales, 4584
Marital Satisfaction Questionnaire, 3027
Marital Satisfaction Scale, 3028, 4585
Marital Transgression Scale, 4586
Market Dissatisfaction Scale, 2645
Marking Speed Test, 1610
Marlowe-Crowne Social Desirability Scale, 57, 449, 2585, 4036 [See also Crowne-Marlowe Social Desirability Scale; Social Desirability Scale]

Marlowe Crowne Social Desirability Scale—Short Form, 4037, 5795

Marlowe-Crowne Social Desirability Test—Adapted, 450

Marriage Adjustment Scale, 648 [See also Marital Adjustment Scale]

Marriage and Family Questionnaire, 1161

Married Students' Counseling Needs Questionnaire, 1349

Marshall Self-Disclosure Questionnaire, 593

Martin-Larsen Approval Motivation Scale, 2586

Marxist Work Beliefs Scale, 7233, 7234 [See also Work Beliefs Scale]

Masculine-Feminine Semantic Differential, 114

Masculine Gender Identity Scale, 3403

Masculine Gender-Role Stress Questionnaire, 3877

Masculine Rating Scale, 288

Masculinity/Femininity of Self Concept Measure, 795

Masculinity Scale, 7094

Masher Guilt Scale, 289

Maslowian Assessment Survey, 4038

Mastery and Performance Scales, 3713

Mastery Scale, 6793

Masturbation Attitude Scale, 4302

Matching Familiar Figures Test, 290, 291, 942, 2272

Matching Familiar Figures Test—Revised, 1494, 2170

Maternal Behavior Scale, 4587

Maternal Risk for Depressive Symptomatology—Questionnaire Form, 5586

Maternal Separation Anxiety Scale, 4588, 6465

Maternal Variables, 2273

Math Anxiety Measure, 3714

Math Anxiety Questionnaire, 3715

Math Problems Performance Scale, 5381

Math/Science Interests Form, 7096

Math-Science Utility Scale, 7235

Math Self-Concept and Learning Scales, 3722

Math Self-Concept Scale, 6798

Math Self-Efficacy Scale, 6799

Mathematical Self-Concept Questionnaire, 3247

Mathematics Achievement Questionnaire, 3244

Mathematics Achievement Test, 2383, 5380

Mathematics Anxiety Rating Scale, 394, 3718

Mathematics Anxiety Rating Scale—Revised, 2417

Mathematics Anxiety Scale, 1630, 3716, 3717, 5416

Mathematics Anxiety Scale (College), 2418

Mathematics Anxiety Scale for Children, 3719

Mathematics as a Male Domain Scale, 3245

Mathematics Attitude Scale, 524, 2761, 2762

Mathematics Attitude Scales, 6144

Mathematics Attitude Survey, 6145, 6146

Mathematics Attribution Scale, 3246, 4875

Mathematics Course Interests Scale, 7095

Mathematics Course Outcome Expectations Scale, 6794

Mathematics Efficacy Scales, 3720

Mathematics Learning in the Classroom Questionnaire, 4303

Mathematics Motivation and Attitudes Scales, 3721

Mathematics Self-Concept Scale, 1409, 3248

Mathematics Self-Efficacy—College Courses Scale—Revised, 6797

Mathematics Self-Efficacy Scale, 3249, 4876, 6795

Mathematics Self-Efficacy Scale (Japanese Version), 4877

Mathematics Self-Efficacy Scale—Revised, 6796

Mathematics Semantic Differential Scales, 525

Mathis et al. Semantic Differential, 115

Matthews Youth Test for Health, 3489, 4414, 5193

Matthews Youth Test for Health (MYTH-Form O), 1869

Maturity of Career Choice Scale, 5333

Maturity of Moral Judgment Scale, 2218

Maudsley Obsessive Compulsive Inventory, 7025

Mayo Task Reaction Questionnaire—Modified, 3140

Maze Test, 2847

McClelland Thematic Apperception Test of n-Achievement (n-Ach), 726 [See also N Ach TAT]

McClelland's Need Achievement Thematic Apperception Test, 727 [See also N Ach TAT]

McClosky Conservatism Scale, 1518

McCroskey and Jenson Source Credibility Scale, 6348

McGill Pain Questionnaire, 4415

McGuire and White Socioeconomic Status Scale, 899

McKinney Sentence Completion Blank, 796

McQuary-Truax Underachievement Scale, 1069

McReynolds Success Failure Inventory, 526 [See also Success-Failure Inventory]

ME Scale, 3250, 6803

Meaning and Value of Work Scale, 2307

Meaning of Work Scale, 6800

Means-Ends Beliefs Scale, 4878

Means-Ends Problem-Solving Test, 3433, 5139

Measure of Achieving Tendency, 2274

Measure of Elementary Communication Apprehension, 2917

Measure of Epistemological Reflection, 4506

Measure of Inflectional Performance, Revised, 17

Measure of Ingratiatory Behaviors in Organizational Settings, 5977

Measure of Job Satisfaction, 5978 [See also Job Satisfaction Measure]

Measure of Perceived Union Instrumentality, 7395

Measure of Values, 2308 [See also Pierce's Measure of Values]

Measures of Temperament, 5055

Mechanistic Structural Job Characteristics Scales, 3088

Mechanization Scale, 1162

Medical Career Development Inventory, 3640

Medical Career Self-Efficacy Scales, 6801

Medical School Environmental Stress Inventory, 2419

Medical Schools Learning Environment Survey, 3089

Medical Social Desirability Scale, 5796

Medical Student Self-Confidence Scale, 4879

Mehrabian Achievement Scale, 1350

Mehrabian Achieving-Tendency Scale, 2006 [See also Achieving Tendency Scales for Males and Females]

Mehrabian and Bank Achievement Questionnaire, 3141

Mehrabian and Epstein Emotional Empathy Scale, 3490 [See also Emotional Empathy Scale]

Mehrabian Resultant Achievement Motivation Scales, 728 [See also Resultant Achievement Motivation Test—Short Form]

Meichenbaum—Instrument to Assess Attitude toward Academic Factors, 527

Meier Burnout Assessment, 2420, 2646, 3723

Melbourne Pain Apperception Test, 2095

Member Liking of the Leader Scale, 5797

Member-Perceived Similarity with Leader Scale, 6802

Member View of Leader-Member Exchange Scale, 6349 [See also Leader-Member Exchange Scale—Member Form]

Member's Performance Scale, 6259

Memory Assessment Questionnaire, 2384

Memory Check, 2385

Memory for Semantic Classes, 358

Memory for Semantic Implications, 359

Memory for Semantic Transformations Tests, 11

Memory for Semantic Units, 360

Memory for Symbolic Classes, 361

Memory for Symbolic Implications, 116, 362

Memory for Symbolic Transformations Test, 117

Memory for Symbolic Units, 363

Memory Impairment Scale, 2386

Men's Adult Life Experiences Inventory, 4507

Menstrual Distress Questionnaire—Dutch, 3880

Mental Development Scales, 2956

Mental Dexterity Test, 1738, 6055 [See also Thumin Test of Mental Dexterity]

Mental Health Inventory, 2493, 3878, 5587

Mental Health Locus of Control Scale, 2096

Mental Health Locus of Origin Scale, 1801

Mental Health Scale, 3879

Mental Health Values Questionnaire, 7236

Mental Imagery Questionnaire, 4880 [See also Betts Questionnaire upon Mental Imagery—Revised]

Mental, Physical, and Spiritual Well-Being Scale, 5588

Mental Retardation Preference Scale, 7097

Mental Rotations, 3680

Mental Rotations Test, 2097

Mentor-Protege Relationship Questionnaire, 7308

Mentor Scale, 7309

Mentoring Functions Scale, 7307

Mentoring Functions Scales, 5289

Mentorship vs. Supervisory Relationship Scales, 7310

Merit Pay Attitude Scale, 4304

Meritocracy Scale, 6578

Met Expectations of Job Scale, 5979

Metacognitive Questionnaire, 6056

Meta-Regulation and Evaluation Scales, 5589

Michigan Organizational Assessment Questionnaire—Adapted, 5980

Michigan Student Questionnaire, 1163

Michill Adjective Rating Scale, 1410

Microcomputer Attitude Scale, 4305

Microcounseling Skill Discrimination Scale, 2351

Middle School Questionnaire, 1326

[Middlesex] Hospital Questionnaire, 3849

Mikulecky Behavioral Reading Attitude Measure, 2763

Militancy Scale, 1495

Military Morale Scale, 1971

Miller Social Intimacy Scale, 2587, 5798 [See also Social Intimacy Scale]

Miller's Locus-of-Control Scale, 797

Milwaukee School Guidance Evaluation Scale, 687

Mines-Jensen Interpersonal Relationship Inventory, 2588

Mines-Jensen Interpersonal Relationships Inventory, 5799

Minimal Reading Proficiency Assessment, 1611

Mini-Markers, 7026

Mini-Mental State Test, 5590

Minimum Proficiency Skills Test, 3681

Miniscat Test, 1932

Minnesota Importance Questionnaire (MIQ), 323, 4163

Minnesota Job Description Questionnaire, 4164

Minnesota Satisfaction Questionnaire, 4165, 4166

Minnesota School Affect Assessment, 1802

Minnesota Therapy Rating Scale, 3090

Mirenda Leisure Interest Finder, 3404

Misfortune Attribution Scale, 4881

Mississippi Scale for Combat-Related Post-Traumatic Stress Disorder, 3881

Missouri Children's Behavior Checklist, 1870

Missouri College English Test, 364

Missouri Comprehensive Guidance Evaluation Survey, 6804

MIST Test (Motoric Ideational Sensory Test), 594

MMPI Women's Scholastic Personality Scale, 1119, 1739

Mobility Inventory for Agoraphobia, 3882, 3883

Modern Life Scale, 4656

Modern Racism Scale, 5800, 6147

Modern Value Orientation Index, 976

Modernism Index, 302

Modernity Attitude Scale, 4306

Modernity Measure, 1327

Modernity Scale, 1164, 1165, 2309

Modes of Problem-Solving Scale, 7134

Modified Erikson Psychosocial Stage Inventory, 4514 [See also Erikson Psychosocial Stage Inventory—Revised]

Modified Fear Survey, 3884 [See also Fear Survey ...]

Modified Hall's Matrices, 1740

Modified Interpersonal Relationship Scale, 5801 [See also Interpersonal Relationship Scale]

Modified Personal Involvement Inventory, 5092 [See also Personal Involvement Inventory; Revised Personal Involvement ...]

Modified Role Repertory Test, Adapted, 1465, 2203

Modified Scale for Suicidal Ideation, 5591 [See also Scale for Suicide Ideation; Suicide Ideation Scale]

Modifiers and Perceived Stress Scale, 3885

Modular-Flexible Schedule Questionnaire, 1328

Money Attitude Scale, 2764

Mood Adjective Checklist, 1496 [See also Nowlis-Green Mood Adjective Checklist]

Mood Check List, 3886

Mood Questionnaire, 2494

Mood Questionnaire (Shortened Version), 1669

Mood Scale, 416, 1083

Mood Survey, 2275, 5592

Moral Commitment Scale, 3541

Moral Content Components Test, 3542
Moral Development Scale, 2957
Moral Development Test, 139
Moral Indexes, 977
Moral Judgment Interview, 2310, 5140
Moral Judgment Measure, 1519
Moral Judgment Scale, 2219, 3543 [See also Kohlberg's Moral Judgment Scale]
Moral Judgment Test, 2311
Moral Judgments in Mitigating Circumstances Scale, 852
Moral Orientation Questionnaire, 7237
Moral Orientation Scale Using Childhood Dilemmas, 5232
Moral Values Rating Scale, 978
Morale Scale, 2495, 2496 [See also Philadelphia Geriatric Center Morale Scale]
Morningness Scale, 7183, 7184
Morphographic Transfer Test, 2387
Morrow Assessment of Nausea and Emesis, 4416
Morrow College Major Satisfaction Questionnaire, 872
Mosaic Construction Test, 611
Mosher Record Choice Guilt Scale, 2276
Most Like Questionnaire, 798
Most Unpleasant Concept Test, 35
Mother-Child Affectionate Interaction Scale, 1953
Mother-Child Interaction Scale, 649
Mother-Daughter Conflict Scale, 6467
Mother-Daughter Relationship Scale, 6468
Mother-Father-Peer Scale: Maternal Acceptance Subscale, 4589
Mother's Attitude toward Deviance, 1803
Mother's Controls and Regulations Scale, 1954
Mother's Interaction Index, 1300

Mother's Religiosity, 2312
Mother's Traditional Beliefs Scale, 2313
Motion Picture Test of Perceptual Abilities, 2098
Motion Sickness Questionnaire, 2848
Motivated Strategies for Learning Questionnaire, 4882
Motivating Potential Score, 3091
Motivation Assessment Scale, 4718, 6654
Motivation Check-Sheet, 1351
Motivation for Marriage Scale, 4719
Motivation to Avoid Appearing Incompetent Scale, 1352
Motivation to Change Scale—Modified, 4720
Motivation to Learn Scale, 6655
Motivation to Shop Scales, 4883
Motivation to Train for New Technologies Scale, 4721
Motor Activity Anxiety Test, 5593
Motor Inhibition Test, 59
Motor Perceived Competence Scale, 6805
Mottola History of Interpersonal Distance Scale, 451
Movies Attitude Scale, 1166, 2765
Moving Slot Motion Picture Test, 1411
Multi-Alcoholic Personality Inventory Scale, 2849
Multicultural Counseling Awareness Scale, 6807
Multicultural Counseling Inventory, 7311
Multi-Dimensional Aggression Scale, 2277
Multidimensional Anger Inventory, 7185
Multidimensional Body-Self Relations Questionnaire, 6806
Multidimensional Fear of Death Scale, 2497
Multidimensional Health Locus of Control Scale, 3251, 4884

Multidimensional Health Locus of Control Scales, 6808

Multidimensional Job Satisfaction Scale, 4167

Multidimensional Locus of Control Scale, 6809

Multidimensional Locus of Pain Control Questionnaire, 6810

Multidimensional Measure of Children's Perceptions of Control, 3252, 6811

Multidimensional-Multiattributional Causality Scale, 3253, 6812

Multidimensional Perfectionism Scale, 7186, 7187

Multidimensional Personality Questionnaire, 5056, 5057

Multidimensional Personality Questionnaire—Negative Emotionality, 7027

Multidimensional Racial Identity Scale, 5802

Multidimensional Rating Scale, 5141

Multidimensional Scale of Perceived Social Support, 4039

Multi-Dimensional Scale of Political Preference, 873

Multidimensional Sense of Humor Scale, 6368

Multidimensional Sexuality Questionnaire, 5594

Multidimensional Social Decentering Scale, 5803

Multidimensional Support Scale, 5804

Multifactor Leadership Questionnaire, 4417, 6261

Multifactor Racial Attitude Inventory, 87 [See also Woodmansee-Cook Multifactor Racial Attitude Inventory]

Multifactor Racial Attitude Inventory—Revised, 1804

Multigroup Ethnic Identity Measure, 5805, 5806

Multimethod Job Design Questionnaire, 3092, 6579

Multimethod Job Design Questionnaire: Self-Report, 4657

Multiple Choice Bender Test, 1412

Multiple Item Appraisal Form, 3587

Multiple Role Stress Scale, 5595

Multiple Sclerosis Incapacity Scale, 3887

Multiple Stimulus Types Ambiguity Tolerance—1, 7188

Multiracial Attitude Questionnaire (MAQ), 2766

Multiscore Depression Inventory, 1670

Multiscore Depression Inventory—Short Form, 2498, 2534

Multi-Task Behavioral Avoidance Task, 5596

Multi-Trait Personality Inventory, 7028

Multivariate Achievement Predictor Test, 2683

Music Control Scale, 5981

Mutilated Words Test, 1612

Mutuality of Autonomy Scale, 4508

My Class Inventory, 3093, 3094, 4658

My Class Inventory—Modified, 6580

My Education, 4723

My Education Scale, 4722

Myers Achievement Motivation Scale, 729 [See also Achievement Motivation Scale]

Myrick Semantic Differential, 118 [See also Semantic Differential]

Mysticism Scale, 3544, 6262

Mysticism Scale (Form D), 4418

N

N Ach TAT, 204 [See also McClelland...; McClelland's...]

NachNaff Scale, 2007, 3142, 6652
Narcissism Inventory, 5194
Narcissistic Injury Scale, 7189
Narcissistic Personality Disorder
  Scale, 5195
Narcissistic Personality Inventory,
  3491, 5196–5198, 7190, 7191
Narcissistic Personality Inven-
  tory—Revised, 5199
Narrative Job Description Classifi-
  cation System, 3095
Native American Value-Attitude
  Scale, 3545
Nature-Nurture Attribution Scale,
  4885
Nature of Epistemological Beliefs
  Scale, 3546
Navy Equal Opportunity/Sexual
  Harassment Survey, 6263
Nebraska Skill Analysis System,
  1897
Necessary Facts Test, 2220
Need Assessment Questionnaire,
  1329
Need-Desire Instrument, 2008
Need for Academic Competence
  Scale, 2421
Need-for-Achievement Scale, 1353,
  2009, 4724, 6656–6658
Need for Autonomy Scale, 2010
Need for Clarity Index, 2647
Need for Cognition Scale, 3367,
  4725, 4726, 5142, 7030
Need for Cognition Scale—Dutch
  Version, 7029
Need for Cognition Scale (Short
  Form), 4727
Need Satisfaction in Nonwork
  Settings Scale, 4728
Need Satisfaction Scale, 2011, 2012,
  3143
Need Satisfaction Schedule, 2013
Needs of Adolescent Runaways,
  6264
Negation Elicitation Scale, 2933
Negative Administrative Stereo-
  types Questionnaire, 528

Negative Affectivity Scale, 3888,
  5597
Negative Assertion Questionnaire,
  3492
Negative Mood Index, 5598
Negative Mood Regulation Scale,
  3889, 5599
Negative Mood Scale, 3890
Negative Self-Evaluation Scale,
  4886
Negative Well-Being Scale, 2499
Negotiating Latitude Scales, 2918
Negro-White Student Friendship
  Questionnaire, 452
NEO Inventory, 3496
Neophilia Scale, 5093
Nettler's Alienation Scale, 453
Network Orientation Scale, 2589,
  5807
Neuropsychiatric Hospital Suicide
  Potential Scale, 1671
Neurotic Manifestations, 36
Neurotic Trait Screening Scale,
  3891
Neutral Objects Satisfaction
  Questionnaire, 5600, 5601
"New Father" Role Scale, 6469
New Left Scale, 1520
New Racism Scale, 5808
New Scientific Uses Test, 1933
New York University Occupational
  Choice Questionnaire, 1587
Newspaper Recognition Checklist,
  5382
Newtonian Mechanics Word-
  association Test, 119
Niederhoffer Police Cynicism Scale,
  943
Noise Sensitivity Scale, 2099, 2850,
  3110, 3892
Non-Cognitive Questionnaire, 2684,
  3724, 4228, 6813
Non-Cognitive Questionnaire—
  Revised, 3725
Nonconformity Scale, 4040
Nonpathological Compulsiveness
  Scale, 3493

nonProtestant Ethic Scale, 7238
Nonresidential Father's Parenting Scale, 6470
Nonsexist Personal Attribute Inventory for Children, 3254
Nonsexual Experience Sensation Seeking Scale, Revised, 6659
Nonverbal Applicant Rating Scale, 3588
Nonverbal Communication Questionnaire, 6350
Nonwork Influences of Job Attrition, 4168
Norbeck Social Support Questionnaire, 4041
NORC Occupational Prestige Scale, 900 [See also Occupational Prestige Scale]
Normative Commitment Scales, 5334
Normative Patterns Scales, 7312
Normlessness Scale, 454
North-Hatt-NORC Occupational Prestige Questionnaire, Modification of, 273
Novaco Anger Inventory—Revised, 3494 [See also Anger Inventory]
Novel Maturity Scale, 1053
Novelty-Experiencing Scale, 2187, 6660
Nowicki-Strickland Children's Internal-External Control Scale, 3183
Nowicki-Strickland Children's Locus of Control—Modified Scale, 2101
Nowicki-Strickland Internal-External Control Scale for Adults, 3255 [See also Adult Nowicki-Strickland...; Adult Version of the Nowicki-Strickland...; Nowicki-Strickland Locus of Control Scale for Adults]

Nowicki-Strickland Internal External Control Scale for Early Elementary Children, 4888 [See also Preschool and Primary Nowicki-Strickland...]
Nowicki-Strickland Locus of Control Scale, 799, 4887, 6814 [See also Locus of Control Scale for Children]
Nowicki-Strickland Locus of Control Scale for Adults, 1413, 2100 [See also Adult Nowicki-Strickland...; Adult Version of the Nowicki-Strickland...; Nowicki-Strickland Internal-External Control Scale for Adults]
Nowicki-Strickland Personal Reaction Survey, 2102
Nowlis-Green Mood Adjective Checklist, 417 [See also Mood Adjective Checklist]
Noxious Physical Environment Scale, 4659
Nuclear Activism Questionnaire, 4419
Nuclear Attitudes Questionnaire, 4307
Nuclear Likelihood Questionnaire, 4889
Nuclear Locus of Control Scales, 4890
Number Series, 2221
Nurse Stress Inventory, 4169
Nurses' Attitudes toward Arthritis Scale, 2767
Nurses Training Experiences Scale, 4660
Nursing Commitment Scale, 7396
Nursing Course Attractiveness Scale, 3641
Nursing Role Conflict Scale, 4170
Nursing Satisfaction Scale, 4171
Nursing Stress Scale, 2648, 5982
Nurturance Rating Task, 4590
Nutritional Locus of Control, 4891

O

Obedience Test, 60

Oberleder Attitude Scale, 4308

Object and Person Permanence Scale, 140

Object Classification Test, 1224

Object Relations and Reality Testing Inventory, 5602 [See also Bell Object Relations-Reality Testing Inventory]

Object Relations Inventory, 5603, 5809 [See also Bell Object Relations Inventory]

Object Scale, 635

Object Sorting Test, 1273

Objective and Subjective Burden Scales, 4042

Objective Marital Dependency Measure, 3029

Objective Moral Judgment Scale, 2222

Objectivism Scale, 5058

Obscene Word Semantic Differential, 1274

Observation Schedule and Record, 574

Obsessive-Compulsive Scale, 3497, 3893

Obsessive Thoughts Questionnaire, 5604

Occupation Analysis Inventory, 3096

Occupation Auction, 2314

Occupational Age Questionnaire, 4661

Occupational Alternatives Questionnaire, 7397

Occupational Aspiration Scale, 901, 3447 [See also Haller Occupational Aspiration Scale]

Occupational Choice Satisfaction Scale, 5983

Occupational Concept Test, 1909

Occupational Identity Scale, 4509

Occupational Interest Area Indicator, 199

Occupational Introversion-Extroversion, 292

Occupational Inventory, 711

Occupational Life Assessment (Japanese), 5605

Occupational Needs and Values Questionnaire, 7398

Occupational Plans Questionnaire, 5984

Occupational Preference Sex Role Scale, 874

Occupational Prestige Questionnaire, 275

Occupational Prestige Scale, 274 [See also NORC Occupational Prestige Scale]

Occupational Questionnaire, 4172, 6815

Occupational Rating Scale, 3642

Occupational Self-Efficacy Scale, 3256, 6816

Occupational Stress Scale, 2649

Occupational Stress Scales, 5985

Occupational Value Commitment Scale, 7399

Occupational Value Survey, 2315

Occupational Values Scale, 5233

Occupational Values Scales, 2316

O'Connell Story Test, 2278

OCS Stress Reaction Scale, 1672, 1673

O'Donovan Trust Scale, 1497

Off-Job Interference Scale, 5986

Offer's Self Image Questionnaire, 2103

Office Attitude Questionnaire, 3368

Ohio Social Acceptance Scale, 1104

Ohio Work Values Inventory, 2317, 5234

O'Leary-Porter Scale, 4591, 6446, 6471

Olguin Diagnostic Test of Auditory Perception, 1613

Oliver & Butcher Survey of Opinions about Education, 529

Omnibus Test, 6817
Onomatopoeia and Images, 1281
Ontario Problem Assessment
Battery, 1674
Ontario Test of Intrinsic Motiva-
tion, 730
Open Office Opinion Inventory,
1805
Open Processing Scale, 4729
Open Processing Style Scale, 3369
Openness about Mental Illness
Scale, 530
Openness to Experience Inventory,
4485
Opinion Leadership Scale, 2104
Opinion Leadership Scale—
Revised, 6265
Opinion of Negroes Scale, 88
Opinion Questionnaire on Cultur-
ally and Economically Disadvan-
taged Children & Youth, 531
Opinionnaire on Attitudes toward
Education, 1167
Opinionnaire on Political Institu-
tions and Participation, 1806
Opinions about Deaf People Scale,
6148
Opinions about Mental Illness
Scale, 1807, 6149
Opinions about Psychology Scale,
5094
Opinions about Testing Question-
naire, 6150
Oppositionality Scale, 1225
Oral Multiple Choice Vocabulary
Comprehension Test, 365
Oral P/S Language Inventory, 1275
Oral Reading and Recall Evaluation
Scale, 2388
Organicism-Mechanism Paradigm
Inventory, 7098
Organization Climate Survey
Instrument, 176
Organization Satisfaction Scale,
5988
Organization Work-Family Policies
Scale, 6588

Organizational and Professional
Commitment Scales, 3644 [See
also Organizational Commitment
Scale; Professional Commitment
Scale]
Organizational Attraction Scale,
5335
Organizational Characteristics
Inventory, 4662
Organizational Choice Scale, 2105
Organizational Citizenship Behav-
ior Scale, 2851, 5290, 6266
Organizational Citizenship Behav-
ior Scale—Revised, 6267
Organizational Climate Description
Questionnaire, 688, 4663
Organizational Climate Descriptive
Questionnaire for Middle
Schools, 6581
Organizational Climate Question-
naire, 3097, 6582
Organizational Climate Question-
naire—Revised, 3098
Organizational Climate Scale, 3099
Organizational Commitment and
Satisfaction Inventory, 7400
Organizational Commitment
Questionnaire, 2014, 3643, 5338,
7401–7405
Organizational Commitment
Questionnaire—Adapted, 7406
Organizational Commitment
Questionnaire—Short Form,
5336, 7418
Organizational Commitment Scale,
2015, 2016, 3645–3648, 5337,
5339–5343, 7407–7417 [See also
Organizational and Professional
Commitment Scales]
Organizational Communication
Scale, 1898, 2919
Organizational Conflict Inventory,
5810
Organizational Culture Survey,
6583
Organizational Diversity Inventory,
6584

Organizational Fairness Scale, 4664

Organizational Health Description Questionnaire, 1330

Organizational Health Inventory, 4665

Organizational Identification Scale, 3649, 7419

Organizational Need Satisfaction Scales, 1354

Organizational Practices Questionnaire, 1972

Organizational Readjustment Rating Scale, 2650

Organizational Research Evaluation Scales, 1331

Organizational Socialization Questionnaire, 5987

Organizational Stress Scale, 4666

Organizational Structure Measure, 1332

Organizational Structure Scale, 6585

Organizational Support Scale, 6586

Organizational Value Orientation Questionnaire, 6587, 7239

Orientation to Clothing Index, 875

Orientation to Learning Scale, 3547

Orientation to Life Questionnaire, 5606

Orientation to Literacy Test, 3257

Origin Climate Questionnaire, 3100

Osgood Tannenbaum and Suci Emotionality Scale, 944

Osgood-Tannenbaum-Suci Self Esteem Scale, 800

Osterhouse Test Anxiety Instrument (Modified), 396

Osterhouse Test Anxiety Inventory, 395 [See also Test Anxiety Inventory]

Other Dyadic Perspective-Taking Scale, 4043

Other Esteem Questionnaire, 324

Ottens-Tucker Academic Anxiety Coping Scale, 4420

Outcome Expectancies Questionnaire, 4893

Outcome-Expectations Questionnaire, 4892

Outcome Expectations Scale, 6818

Outcome Questionnaire, 5607

Outcome Values Questionnaire, 5235

Overall Job Satisfaction Scale, 4173–4175

Overall Quality of Life, 5608

Overexcitability Questionnaire, 2852, 3495

Overt Self-Criticism Scale, 6819

Owens Biographical Inventory, 1120

Ozawa Behavioral Rating Scale, 2853

P

Pace Scale of Attitudes toward Married Women's Employment, 4309

Page Fantasy Scale (Worry Score), 945

Pain Behavior Scale, 2854

Paper Form Board Test, 2106

Pappo Fear of Success Scale, 2500

Paragraph Completion Method, 2934

Paragraph Completion Test, 120, 891, 1498, 1499, 1910

Paragraphs about Leisure, 5609

Paranoia Scale, 5610

Parareligious Belief Inventory, 5236

Parent-Adolescent Attachment Inventory, 6472

Parent-Adolescent Communication Scale, 6473

Parent-Adolescent Relationships Scale, 3030

Parent as a Teacher Inventory, 1808

Parent Attitude Questionnaire, 532
Parent Attitude Research Instrument, 144, 533
Parent Attitude Survey (PAS), 3032 [See also Hereford Parent Attitude Survey]
Parent Behavior Checklist, 6483
Parent Behavior Form, 4599
Parent Behavior Scale, 4600
Parent Checklist of Child Behavior, 2856
Parent-Child Affect Scale, 6484
Parent-Child Interaction Rating Scales—Modified, 1955 [See also Heilbrun Parent-Child Interaction Rating Scales]
Parent-Child Relation Questionnaire—Short Form II, 3033 [See also Roe-Siegelman Parent-Child Relations Questionnaire]
Parent-Child Relationship Scales, 4601
Parent-Child Relationship Survey, 3034
Parent-Child Scale, 6485
Parent Daily Report, 6268
Parent Daily Reports, 4602
Parent Opinion Questionnaire, 4607
Parent Participation Interview, 6490
Parent Perception Inventory, 6491
Parent Perceptions Questionnaire, 1956
Parent Questionnaire, 4608
Parent Rating Scale, 1303
Parent Reading Belief Inventory, 6151
Parent School Efficacy Scale, 6821
Parent Somatic Complaints, 5611
Parent Support and Affection Scales, 6493
Parent Temperament Questionnaire, 3370
Parental Acceptance-Rejection Questionnaire, 3031, 4593, 6474
Parental Acceptance Scale, 4592

Parental Attachment Questionnaire, 4594, 6475
Parental Attitudes toward Childrearing, 6476
Parental Authority Questionnaire, 6477, 6478
Parental Behavior Scale, 2855
Parental Bonding Instrument, 4595, 6479
Parental Control Questionnaire, 145
Parental Dominance Scale, 1301
Parental Evaluation of Children's Creativity, 6369
Parental Expectations Survey, 1302
Parental Home Assessment Index, 4596
Parental Interest Scale, 650
Parental Involvement and Child Care Index, 6480
Parental-Leave-Policy Fairness Scale, 6820
Parental Nurturance Scale, 4597, 6481
Parental Relationship Questionnaire, 6482
Parental Satisfaction with Their Child Scale, 4598
Parental Stress Scale, 3894
Parenting Control Scale, 5743
Parenting Daily Hassles Scale, 4603, 6486
Parenting Inventory, 6487
Parenting Q-Sort, 4605
Parenting Questionnaire, 4604
Parenting Scales, 6488
Parenting Sense of Competence Scale, 4606
Parenting Styles Questionnaire, 6489
Parents and Friends Scale, Adapted, 5706
Parents' Attitudes toward Unions, 6152
Parents' Beliefs about Cholesterol, 6492

Parents' Participation in Unions, 6822

Parten's Social Participation Scale, 5811

Participation in Decision-Making Index, 4176

Participation Motivation Questionnaire, 6661

Participative Decision-Making Scale, 7135

Passionate Love Scale, 5812

Passive-Aggressive Behavior Scale, 6269

Pathological Behavior Rating Scale, 1226

Patient Adjustment Q Sort Technique, 418

Patient Behavior Test, 1871

Patient Satisfaction Interview, 6589

Patient Self-Disclosure Instrument—Importance Scale, 4486

Patient Sick-Role Scale, 3895

Patient Stress Behavior Index, 5613

Patients' Coping Strategies after Surgery Scale, 5612

Patrolman's Work Role Questionnaire, 257

Pattern Copying Test, 801

Pay Cognitions Scale, 5989

Pay Expectation Scale, 3258

Pay Freeze Hardship Scale, 5990

Pay Increase Scale, 2651

Pay Satisfaction Questionnaire, 4177, 5991

Pay Satisfaction Scale, 2652, 4178

Pay Valence Scale, 6662

Peak Communications Experiences Scales, 2920

Peak Performance and Peak Experience Questionnaire, 4421

Pearlin-Rosenberg Status Distance Scale—Modified, 902

Pearson-Maddi Similes Preference Inventory—Revised, 1054 [See also Similes Preference Inventory]

Pediatric Pain Questionnaire, 2857

Peer Adjustment Index, 5813

Peer and Family Scales, 6494

Peer Classroom Performance Rating Scale, 575

Peer Counseling Consumer Satisfaction Questionnaire, 7313

Peer Counseling Helping Style Questionnaire, 6823

Peer Counseling Outcome Measure, 1973

Peer-Directed Behavior Observation, 4422

Peer Drug Associations Scale, 4423

Peer Evaluation and Preference Test, 1168

Peer Group Orientation Scale, 534

Peer Network Functions Scale, 2591

Peer Nomination Inventory of Depression (PNID), 2502, 3896

Peer Rating Depression Scale, 2503

Peer Rating Index of Aggression, 946, 3498

Peer Rating of Personality Traits Scale, 3499

Peer Ratings Semantic Differential, 802

Peer Relationship Satisfaction Scale, 4044

Peer Role-Taking Questionnaire, 3259

Peer Social Support Scale, 4045

Peer Support Scale for Teachers, 4046

Pejorative Epithet Scale, 2858

Penn State Worry Questionnaire, 7192

Pensacola Z Scale, 1500

People Knowing Questionnaire, 3897

People Test, 535

Perceived Academic Ability Scale, 6824

Perceived Academic Success Scale, 5417

Perceived Adequacy of Resources Scale, 6495

Perceived Behavioral Control Scale, 6270

Perceived Client Sensitivity to Loss Scale, 5614

Perceived Climate Questionnaire—Revised, 4667

Perceived Clothing Deprivation Questionnaire, 4894

Perceived Cognitive Competence Questionnaire, 6825

Perceived Competence Scale for Children, 3260, 4895, 6762, 6826

Perceived Confirmation Scale, 3261

Perceived Conflict Inventory, 4896

Perceived Control at School Scale, 4897

Perceived Control over Time Scale, 6827

Perceived Control Questionnaire, 6828

Perceived Control Scale, 6829–6832, 7314

Perceived Decoding Ability Scale—Form 1, 5814

Perceived Depth of Interaction Scale, 1722, 1899

Perceived Economic Status, 5161

Perceived Family Problems Scale, 6496

Perceived Fraudulence Scale, 6833

Perceived Guilt Index, 2279

Perceived Influence Scale, 2653

Perceived Internal Control, 6834

Perceived Job Control, 5992

Perceived Life Satisfaction Scale, 5615

Perceived Marital Satisfaction Index, 3035

Perceived Maternal Encouragement Measure, 651

Perceived Maternal Warmth Questionnaire, 652

Perceived Need-Deficiency Scale, 1355

Perceived Opportunities for Exercise Questionnaire, 4898

Perceived Organizational Support Scale, 6590, 6591

Perceived Parental Rearing Practices Scales, 4609

Perceived Parenting Questionnaire, 1304

Perceived Participation Scale, 3262

Perceived Paternal Parenting Scales, 3036

Perceived Performance Scale, 6835

Perceived Personal Competency Rating Scale, 6836

Perceived Physical Activity Scale, 6837

Perceived Physical Competence Scale, 6838

Perceived Physical Fitness Scale, 4899

Perceived Product Knowledge Scale, 6839

Perceived Quality of Academic Life Scale, 4668

Perceived Quality of Classroom's Physical Environment Instrument, 6592

Perceived Quality Scale, 6593

Perceived Relatedness to Peers Questionnaire, 6840

Perceived Security Scale, 3037

Perceived Self-Efficacy Scale, 4900, 6841, 6842

Perceived Self-Need for Improvement, 6843

Perceived Self Questionnaire, 4510

Perceived Self-Worth Questionnaire, 6844

Perceived Social Support—Family Scale, 4610

Perceived Social Support: Friends Scale, 4047

Perceived Social Support from Family and Friends Scales, 6497

Perceived Social Support Scale, 5815, 5993

Perceived Somatotype Scale, 3263

Perceived Soviet Threat, 4901

Perceived Sport Ability Scale, 6845

Perceived Stress Scale, 2501, 3898, 5616
Perceived Supervisor Credibility Semantic Differential, 1556
Perceived Teacher Behavior Inventory, 6271
Perceived Teacher Support of Questioning Scale, 5418
Perceived Understanding Scale, 3264
Perceived Union Support Scale, 6594
Perceived Work Alternatives Scale, 4179, 6846
Perceived Work Load Scale, 4180
Perceived Workload Index, 5994
Perception of Child Psychologist Questionnaire, 3265
Perception of Classroom Behavior Scale, 1227
Perception of College Environment Rating Scale, 177
Perception of Counselor Behaviors Questionnaire, 4902
Perception of Interpersonal Hostility Scale, 146
Perception of Interviewer Credibility, 803
Perception of Marital Interaction Scale, 240
Perception of Power Scale, 6847
Perception of Social Closeness Scale, 1723
Perception of Teasing Scale, 5816
Perceptions of Cheating Scale, 6848
Perceptions of Classroom Instructor Scales, 3589
Perceptions of Counselor's Expected Helpfulness, 5291
Perceptions of Discrimination against Blacks Scale, 5817
Perceptions of Discrimination against Women Scale, 5818
Perceptions of Mexican-Americans Scale, 2768
Perceptions of Organizational Politics Scales—Revised, 6596
Perceptions of Parental Beliefs Concerning Teachers, 4903
Perceptions of Sexually Inappropriate Behavior and Intimidation Scales, 6849
Perceptions of Student Misbehavior Scale, 2859
Perceptions of the New Job's Attributes Scale, 6595
Perceptive Listening Test, 2389
Perceptual Aberration Scale, 3266
Perceptual Acuity Test, 2685
Perceptual Indicators of Family Quality of Life Scale, 6498
Perceptual Preferences and Sensitiveness among Environmental Sensory Stimuli Check List—Revised, 5095
Perceptual Test Battery, 1414
Perfectionism Scale, 5200, 7193
Performance Appraisal Discomfort Scale, 5995
Performance Attributions Scale, 6850
Performance Effectiveness Scale, 5292
Performance Evaluation Scale, 5293
Performance Expectancy Scale, 3267
Performance Improvement Guide, 3590
Performance Index, 636
Performance Judgment Scale, 7315
Performance-Maintenance Scales, 6272
Performance of Guidance Functions Rating Scale, 325
Performance Rating Scales, 1557
Performance Self-Attribution Scale, 3268
Performance Self-Esteem Scale, 4904–4906, 6851
Perinatal Grief Scale—Short Version, 3899
Permeability of Boundaries Scale, 4611

Persistence Scale for Children, 5059, 6663

Person Perception Questionnaire, 5066, 6856

Personal Adjustment Behavior Rating Scales, 37

Personal and Academic Self-Concept Inventory, 4907

Personal Anticipations Questionnaire, 2107

Personal Assessment of Intimacy in Relationships Inventory, 2592

Personal Attitude Survey, 6852

Personal Attribute Inventory, 1809, 2108, 2171, 3269, 4669 [See also Revised Personal Attribute Inventory]

Personal Attribute Inventory for Children, 2109, 3270

Personal Attributes Questionnaire, 3271, 5060, 5096–5098, 6853, 6854, 7031

Personal Attributes Question-naire—Short Form, 2110, 4908, 7099

Personal Authority in the Family System Questionnaire, Version C, 6597

Personal Beliefs Scale, 7240

Personal Characteristics Inventory, 7032, 7033 [See also Inventory of Personal Characteristics #7]

Personal Competence Inventory, 1105

Personal Computer Use Attitude Scale, 4310

Personal Control Scale, 3272

Personal Coping Scale, 5617

Personal Dynamics Profiles, 3273

Personal Efficacy Scale, 1415

Personal Feelings Questionnaire—2, 5061

Personal Feelings Scales, 804

Personal Future Extension Test, 805

Personal Future Time Perspective, 806

Personal History Inventory for Children, 3038

Personal History Questionnaire, 1017

Personal, Home, Social, Formal Relations Questionnaire, 1106

Personal Illness-Accidents Scale, 6273

Personal Incentives for Exercise Questionnaire, 4730, 6664

Personal Incentives for Exercise Questionnaire—Version 1, 4731

Personal Interaction Questionnaire, 4048

Personal Involvement Inventory, 5101, 7100 [See also Modified Personal Involvement...; Revised Personal Involvement...]

Personal Life Satisfaction Scale, 2504

Personal Maturity Scale, 4511

Personal Need Scales, 1356

Personal Opinion Study, 853

Personal Opinion Survey, 612

Personal Orientation Inventory, 979

Personal Philosophy Inventory, 5143

Personal Powers Scale, 6855

Personal Problems Inventory—Modified, 5619

Personal Questionnaire, 419

Personal Reaction Scale, 3274, 4909

Personal Relationship Maintenance Difficulty Scale, 4049

Personal Religiosity Inventory, 5237, 7241

Personal Report of Communication Apprehension, 6351

Personal Resource Questionnaire—Part II, 4050

Personal Responsibility Scale, 5065

Personal Safety Questionnaire, 3682

Personal-Social Adjustment Rating Scales, 397

Personal Space Measure, 1107

Personal Sphere Model, 3548
Personal Strain Questionnaire, 4181
Personal Style Inventory, 3371
Personal Style Inventory—Revised, 5620
Personal Styles Scale, 5621
Personal Support Scale, 5819
Personal Teaching Efficacy Scale, 4910
Personal Values Inventory, 1521
Personal Views Survey, 5622, 5623
Personality Adjustment Questionnaire, 5618
Personality Attributes Questionnaire—Femininity Scale, 5099
Personality Attributes Questionnaire—Masculinity Scale, 5100
Personality Data Form, 2505
Personality Disorder Examination, 5062, 7034
Personality Inventory Scales, 7035
Personality Priorities Inventory for Adolescents, 5063
Personality Rating Scale, 854
Personality Stress Inventory, 3900
Personality Style Scale, 5201
Personality Trait Inferences Test, 2280
Personality Trait Rating Scale, 5064
Personnel Decision Simulation, 2223
Personnel Managers' Attitudes Scale, 1169
Personnel Satisfaction Questionnaire, 178
Perspective Taking, Empathic Concern, and Personal Distress Scale, 7194
Perspective-Taking Scale, 5820
Pet Attachment and Anthropomorphism Scales, 4051
Peterson Problem Checklist, 1108
Pharisaic Virtue Scale, 1170
Pharmacological Rating Scale, 1228

Phenomenology of Consciousness Inventory, 4911
Philadelphia Geriatric Center Morale Scale, 2506 [See also Morale Scale]
Philadelphia Geriatric Center Morale Scale—Revised, 3901
Phillips Anxiety Test, 947
Phillips School Motivation Scale, 731 [See also School Motivation Scale]
Phillips Symptom Checklist, 1084
Philosophies of Human Nature Scale, 980, 1522
Phoneme-Grapheme and Grapheme-Phoneme Tests, 366
Phonemic Awareness Test, 4512
Phonological Awareness Test, 6057
Physical Activity Attitude Inventory, 1171
Physical Activity Inventory, 6274
Physical Activity Socialization Inventory, 5821
Physical Activity Stereotyping Index, 5102, 6857
Physical and Psychological Stress Scales, 2654 [See also Psychological Stress at Work Scale; Psychological Stress Scale]
Physical Anhedonia Scale, 2507
Physical Appearance Evaluation Scale, 4912
Physical Appearance Related Teasing Scale, 5822
Physical Attractiveness Questionnaire, 6858
Physical Attractiveness Rating Scales, 4913
Physical Attractiveness Scale, 3275
Physical Fitness Expectancy of Reinforcement Scale, 4914
Physical Fitness Locus of Control, 4915
Physical Fitness Self-Efficacy Scale, 4916
Physical Fitness-Value Scale, 5238
Physical Health Complaints, 5624

Physical Health Log, 2860
Physical Impairment Scale, 5996
Physical Intimacy Measure, 3039
Physical Self-Efficacy Scale, 6859, 6860
Physical Self-Esteem Scale, 6861
Physical Symptomatology Scale, 5625
Physical Symptoms Checklist, 5626
Physical Symptoms Inventory, 5627
Physical Symptoms Survey, 5628
Physicians' Reactions to Uncertainty Scales, 5997
Piaget Battery, 474
Piano Performance Anxiety Scale, 2508
Pictorial Piagetian Tasks, 2224
Pictorial Scale of Perceived Competence and Social Acceptance for Young Children, 2593, 4052, 4917
Pictorial Self Concept Scale for Children in Grades K–4, 807
Picture Anxiety Test—Revised, 948
Picture-Frustration Study, 1675 [See also Picture Test of Frustration Response; Rosenzweig Picture-Frustration Study]
Picture Interpretation Task, 1085
Picture Squares Test, 808
Picture Test of Frustration Response, 1229 [See also Picture-Frustration Study]
Picture Test of Sexual Thoughts, 1260
Pierce's Measure of Values, 303 [See also Measure of Values]
Piers-Harris Self-Concept Scale, 3276
Pilot Questionnaire, 1974
Planning Process Quality Questionnaire, 6352
Play Behaviors Observation System, 2861
Play Report, 61, 2862
Playground Skills Test, 5383

Pleasant Events Schedule, 2188, 3101, 3902
Pleasure Capacity Scale, 3903
Pleasure in Childrearing Schedule, 6499
Plural Formation Patterns Test, 367
PM Scale, 131
Polarity Scale, 7242
Police Procedures Test, 3683
Police Stress Survey, 4182
Policemen's Attitudes toward Citizenry Scale, 1810
Policy Decision Making Scale, 5998
Political Activity Scale, 576
Political Attitude Questionnaire, 1172
Political Attitude Scale, 536
Political Attitude Scales, 537
Political Causal Attribution Scale (Quebec), 4918
Political Cynicism Scale, 1975
Political Discontentment Scale, 1976
Political Efficacy Scale, 4919
Political Estrangement Scale, 1977
Political Incapability Scale, 2111
Political Knowledge Test, 368
Political Orientation Questionnaire, 4424
Political Sciences Skills Test, 369
Political Tolerance Scale, 5823
Politico-Economic Conservatism Scale, 2318
Polyphasic Values Inventory, 3549
POP, 1811
Popularity/Behavioral Attribute, 4053
Popularity Scale, 4920
Porter Commitment Scale, 7420 [See also Commitment Scale]
Porter Counseling Inventory, 689
Porter Management Position Questionnaire—Modified, 1588
Porter Need Satisfaction Questionnaire, 1357, 1589

Porter Needs Satisfaction Question-
naire—Revised, 3277
Porter Test of Counselor Attitudes,
89, 1173 [See also Test of
Counselor Attitudes]
Portuguese Vocational Interest
Inventory, 7421
Position Description Question-
naire—Short Form, 3104
Positive Affectivity Scale, 5629
Positive and Negative Affect Scale,
3904, 5630
Positive and Negative Affect
Schedule, 5631
Positive and Negative Affect
Schedule Scales, 5632
Positive Impression Survey, 6275
Positive Life Orientation Test, 5633
Positive Reinforcement Observation
Schedule, 2189
Positive Sex Role Inventory, 5103
Possible Barriers to Management
Entry Scale, 4670
Possible Selves Questionnaire,
6862, 6863
Post College Experience Inventory,
3373
Postcounseling Questionnaire, 147
Post-Hospital Behavior Question-
naire, 1230
Postseparation Parental Conflict
Scale, 6500
Post-Transgression Reaction Scale,
4425
Posttreatment Questionnaire, 1416
Potential and Actual Stressors
Scales, 2655
Potential Grievance Scale, 2656
Potential Interpersonal Competence
Scale, 1724, 1900
Potential Managerial Effectiveness
Scale, 6058
Potential Teacher's Attitude
Questionnaire, 4921
Power Apprehension Scale, 4311
Power Measure, 5999
Power Motivation Scale, 732

Power Motive Questionnaire, 4732
Power Source Scales, 6665
Power Usage Checklist, 1231
Powerlessness Scale, 809, 2112,
4054
Practical Knowledge Test, 5384
Practical Training Observation
Schedule, 2863
Practice Teaching Questionnaire,
690
Pragmatic Classification of Depres-
sion Scale, 420
Preactive Decision Exercises, 3434
Precounseling Goal Checklist, 1358
Predicted Behavior of an Adolescent
Questionnaire, 4426
Predicting Displaced Volume Test,
3435
Predicting Future Events Scale,
4922
Prediction of Aggression and
Dangerousness, 7036
Predictive Index Test, 475
Pre-Employment Clerical Test, 73
Pre-Employment Inquiry Quiz,
1018
Pre-Employment Questionnaire,
241
Preference Education Question-
naire, 200
Preference for Aggression-Condu-
cive Activities Assessment Scale,
2190
Preference for Ideation in Problem
Solving Scale, 5144
Preference for Job Enrichment
Scale, 3405
Preference for Numerical Informa-
tion Scale, 7101
Preference for Solitude Scale, 7102
Preference for Types of Organiza-
tions Scale, 259
Preferred Civil-Liberties Climate
Scale, 5104
Preferred Instructor Characteristics
Scale, 3406

Preferred Organizational Climates Scale, 3102
Pregnancy Belief Scale, 6153
Prejudice Measure, 1174
Preliminary Fear of Success Scale, 1676
Premarital Sexual Permissiveness Scale, 4312
Premenstrual Experience Assessment, 4923
Premorbid Social Competence Scale, 2594
Preoccupative Scale, 6276
Prerace Questionnaire—Modified, 5634
Preschool Achievement Test in Reading, Letter Identification, and Numerical Identification, 12
Preschool and Primary Nowicki-Strickland Internal-External Control Scale, 2113, 4924 [See also Nowicki-Strickland Internal External Control Scale for Early...]
Preschool Behavior Questionnaire, 1872, 4427, 4925
Preschool Interpersonal Problem Solving Test, 892
Preschool Observational Scale of Anxiety, 2509
Preschool Racial Attitude Measure II, 1812–1814
Preschool Reading Attitudes Scale, 4313
Preschool Screener, 1741
Presenter's Qualities Rating Form, 3591
Pressure and Manipulation and Antisocial Acts Scales, 6277
Prestatie Motivatie Test, 2017
Pretraining Self-Efficacy Scale, 6864
Preventive Health Behavior Inventory, 2864
PRF ANDRO Scales, 3294
Primary Appraisal of Smoking Cessation Inventory, 7103

Primary Appraisal Scale, 5635
Primary Communication Inventory, 2921
Primary Essay Tests, 370
Primary Grade Pupil Report, 5294, 7316
Primary Pictorial Self-Esteem Test, 3278
Primary Pupils' Reading Attitude Inventory, 1175
Primary Self-Concept Inventory, 2114, 3279
Primary Self-Concept Scale, 2115
Primary Teacher Questionnaire, 6154
Principal Power Tactics Survey, 4428
Principal Support Scale, 4429
Principal's Authoritarianism Index, 2281
Principal's Data Sheet, 595
Principals' Interview Guide, 1558
Principal's Role in Collective Negotiations Q-sort, 538
Principle-Centered Living Survey, 7243
Print Awareness Test, 2390, 4513
Prison Locus of Control Scale, 6865, 6866
Privacy Questionnaire—Turkish Version, 5824
Privacy Regulation Rating Scale, 4055
Private Collective Self-Esteem Scale, 5825
Private-Public Self-Consciousness Scale, 6867
Private Self-Consciousness Scale, 2510, 7037
Private Self-Consciousness Scale—Icelandic Version, 7038
Proactive Personality Measure, 7039
Problem and Role Projection Scales, 2512
Problem-Attack Behavior Inventory, 1232

Problem Behavior Rating Scale, 2865
Problem Checklist, 3905, 5636
Problem-Focused Style of Coping Scale, 5637
Problem History Scale, 6278
Problem Inventory for Adolescent Girls, 2866
Problem Inventory for Adolescent Girls (Multiple-Choice Version), 2595
Problem Severity Rating Scale, 3906
Problem Situation Inventory, 4430
Problem Solving Flexibility Scale, 893
Problem-Solving Inventory, 3280, 3436–3439, 5145, 7136
Problem-Solving Self-Efficacy Scale, 6666
Problem-Solving Skills Inventory, 2225
Problem-Solving Strategy Survey, 5146
Problem Solving Style Questionnaire, 7137
Problem-Solving Task Inventory, 7138
Procedure Behavior Checklist, 2867
Process Activity Form, 577
Process of Change Questionnaire, 5067, 7317
Process-Reactive Scale, 421
Processes of Change Test, 2511
Procrastination Inventory, 2769, 3281, 4431
Procrastination Inventory—Controllability Scale—Revised, 4802
Procrastination Log, 2868, 2869
Procrastination Scale, 4432, 6279, 6280
Product Preference Scale, 5105
Productivity Gain Measure, 7318
Professional Attitudes Scale, 1815

Professional Commitment Scale, 5344, 5345, 7422, 7423 [See also Organizational and Professional Commitment Scales]
Professional Expectations Scale, 4926
Professional Involvement Scale, 7424
Professional Orientation Scale, 539, 6001
Professional Role Orientation Scale for Pharmacists, 4183
Professional-Supervisory Rating Scale, 327
Professionalism and Research Orientation of Students Inventory, 1816
Professionalism Questionnaire, 326
Professionalism Scale, 5346, 6000
Profiles of Organizational Characteristics, 1333
Prohibited Moral Codes Questionnaire, 981
Project Complexity Checklist, 3103
Project Talent Interest Inventory, 201
Projective Prejudice Test, 1176
Proneness to Disorganization under Stress Rating, 2513
Pronunciation Test, 371
Propensity to Divorce Scale, 4612
Propensity to Leave Index, 3650, 6002
Propensity to Leave Scale, 2657, 4184
Propensity to Stay Scale, 6003
Propensity to Strike Scale, 7425
Proportion Test, 1614
Propositional Logic Test, 5147
Pro-Protestant Ethic Scale, 5239, 7244
Prosocial Behavior Scale, 6281
Protest Situational Attitude Scale, 1817
Protestant Ethic Scale, 2320, 2321, 3551, 5240
Protestant Scale, 3550

Protestant Work Ethic Question-
naire, 7245
Protestant Work Ethic Scale, 2319,
7246, 7247
Proverbs Test, 1818, 5148
Provision of Social Relations Scale,
5826
Psychap Inventory, 5638
Psychiatric Disorder
Conceptualization Scale, 3907
Psychiatric Epidemiology Research
Instrument (PERI), 3908, 5639
Psychiatric Evaluation Form, 2514
Psychiatric Status Schedule, 2515
Psychiatric Symptom Index, 1677
Psychological Birth Order Inven-
tory, 5640
Psychological Climate Scale, 6598
Psychological Differentiation
Inventory, 1417
Psychological Distress Index, 5641
Psychological Distress Inventory,
5419
Psychological Distress Scale, 5642
Psychological Effectiveness Scale,
1449
Psychological Inventory of Person-
ality and Symptoms, 3372
Psychological Inventory of Person-
ality and Symptoms, Alcohol
Abuse Scale, 2802
Psychological Maltreatment
Inventory, 5827
Psychological Medical Inventory,
6353
Psychological Occupations Prestige
Questionnaire, 903
Psychological Reactance Scale,
4433, 4733, 6282
Psychological Screening Inventory,
1725, 5643
Psychological Sense of School
Membership Scale, 5420
Psychological Separation Inventory,
3040, 3909, 3910, 4056, 4613,
5421, 5644, 6501

Psychological Size and Distance
Scale, 5828
Psychological Strain, 6004
Psychological Stress at Work Scale,
2658 [See also Physical and
Psychological Stress Scales]
Psychological Stress Scale, 2517
[See also Physical and Psycho-
logical Stress Scales]
Psychological Well-Being Scale,
5645, 5646
Psychological Well-Being Scales,
3911
Psychology Today Woman and Man
Scale, 1177
Psychopathy Checklist, 3912, 3913
Psychopathy in Criminal Popula-
tions Checklist, 2518
Psychosocial Questionnaire, 904
Psychosocial Stress Scale, 5647
Psychosomatic Complaints Scale,
2516
Psychotherapeutic Interaction
Scales, 328
Psychotherapists' Questionnaire,
6155
Psychotherapy Expectancy Inven-
tory—Revised, 4927, 6872
Psychotherapy Problem Checklist,
2519
Psychotherapy Process Inventory,
2352
Psychotherapy Process Q-Sort, 7319
Public Views of Intelligence
Questionnaire, 6156
Pun Test, 613
Punched Holes Test, 2116
Punitive-Internal Attitudes to
Offenders Scale, 6157
Punitiveness Scale, 2770
Pupil Attitude Checklist, 540
Pupil Attitude Questionnaire, 455
Pupil Behavior Inventory—Revised,
578
Pupil Behavior Patterns Scale, 6283
Pupil Control Behavior, 4434

Pupil Control Ideology Form, 810, 1523, 1819, 2117, 3105, 4314, 4928, 6868
Pupil Control Ideology Scale, 2771, 3282
Pupil Control Ideology Scale—Revised, 3283
Pupil Development Survey, 637
Pupil Disruptive Behavior Scale, 4435
Pupil Evaluation Inventory, 3374
Pupil Observation Report, 811
Pupil Opinion Questionnaire, 541, 1820
Pupil Problem Behavior Inventory, 2191
Pupil Rating Form, 2870
Purdue Elementary Problem Solving Inventory, 894, 1468, 2226
Purdue Home Stimulation Inventory, 4614
Purdue Teacher Opinionnaire, 4185
Purpose-in-Life Test (for the Elderly), 5068
Pursuing-Distancing Scale, 2596

Q

Q-Adjustment Score, 422
Q Sort Adjustment Scale, 1678
Q-Sort Inventory of Parenting Behaviors, 4615
Q-Tags Test of Personality, 3500
Qualitative Social Support Index, 4057
Quality Circle Process Scale, 6284
Quality Marriage Index, 6502
Quality of Instruction Questionnaire, 5295
Quality of Life Measure, 3914
Quality of Life Scale, 3915
Quality of Parent-Child Relationships Scale, 6503

Quality of Same-Sex Relationships Questionnaire, 5829
Quality of School Life Questionnaire, 6599
Quality of Teacher Work Life Survey, 4186
Quality of Work Life Measure, 4187
Quantitative Inventory of Alcohol Disorders, 6285
Quantitative Role Overload Scale, 6005
Quantitative Work Overload Scale, 4188
Quarterly Profile Examination, 5385
Quay Behavior Rating Scales, 855
Quay Case History Scale, 856
Quay Personal Opinion Inventory, 857
Questioning Skill Instrument, 7139
Questionnaire for Instructor Rating, 329
Questionnaire of American Values by 2000 A.D., 1524
Questionnaire of Children's Perception of Their Environment, 179
Questionnaire of Response to Certain Auditory Stimuli, 1233
Questionnaire on Resources and Stress—Friedrich Short Form, 4616
Questionnaire on Stress in Diabetic Patients, 5648
Questionnaire on Student and College Characteristics, 180
Questionnaire on Teacher Attitude toward the Profession, 905
Questionnaire upon Mental Imagery—Revised, 2118 [See also Betts Questionnaire upon Mental Imagery—Revised]
Quick Discrimination Index, 6158

R

RA Life Conflict Scale, 4930
Racial Attitudes Questionnaire, 542
Racial Identity Attitude Scale,
    2772, 2773, 4315, 4316, 5830
    [See also RIAS; White Racial
    Identity Attitude Scale]
Racial Intermarriage Rating Scale,
    90
Racial Preference Instrument, 1459
Racial Self-Esteem Scale, 4929
Racial Semantic Differential, 3448
Racism(s) Scale, 5831
Radicalism-Conservatism Inven-
    tory, 1821
Raising Children Scale, 6504
RAM Scale—Revised, 3552
Ramak Interest Inventory, 3651,
    7426
Ramak Questionnaire, 2369
Rank Behavioral Interaction
    Description System (Revised),
    596
Rape Aversiveness Scale, 4931
Rape Empathy Scale—Revised,
    5202
Rape Myth Acceptance Scale, 4932,
    6159
Rape Responsibility Questionnaire,
    4436
Rape Trauma Knowledge Test,
    3684
Rasmussen's Ego Identity Scale,
    949 [See also Ego Identity Scale]
Rathus Assertion Schedule, 2282
Rathus Assertiveness Scale, 1873
Rathus Assertiveness Scale—
    Swedish Version, 7195
Rathus Assertiveness Schedule,
    5203 [See also Assertiveness
    Schedule]
Rathus Assertiveness Schedule—
    Modified, 3501

Rating of Alter-Competence Scale,
    2922, 5832
Rating Scale for Adults, 2192
Rating Scale for Entry-Level
    Psychiatric Aides, 3592
Rating Scale for Job-Related Work,
    3593
Rating Scale for Kindergarten
    Adjustment, 2422
Rating Scale for Teachers of
    Students, 24
Rating Scale of Child's Actual
    Competence, 3685
Rating Scale of Counselor Effective-
    ness, 1559 [See also Counselor
    Effectiveness Scale]
Rating Student Self-Regulating
    Learning Outcomes, 4933
Ratings of Behavioral Depression,
    2520
Rational Behavior Inventory, 1679,
    1874, 2871, 3284
Rational Behavior Inventory—Low
    Reading Level, 2774
Rational Beliefs Inventory, 4317,
    4934
Rawls' Personal Space Measure,
    1418
Reaction and Adaptation to College
    Test, 5422
Reaction Inventory, 950, 1501,
    2283, 3106 [See also Evans
    Reaction Inventory]
Reaction Inventory—Guilt, 2284
Reaction Measure, 6600
Reaction to Exploration Scale, 7427
Reaction to Skill Assessment, 4671
Reactions to Interracial Situations
    at Work Questionnaire, 6006
Reactions to Off-Campus Cohabita-
    tion, 181
Reactions to Tests, 5423
Reactive Curiosity Questionnaire,
    733
Reactive Object Curiosity Test, 260
Reactivity to Events Scale, 4437

Readiness for Parenting Change Scale, 6505

Readiness for Vocational Planning, Revised Edition, 5347 [See also Gribbons-Lohnes Readiness for Vocational Planning]

Reading and Writing Outcome Expectancy Scale, 3916

Reading and Writing Self-Efficacy Instruments, 3726

Reading Attitude Inventory, 1822

Reading Attitude Scale, 543, 2775 [See also Estes...]

Reading Attitude Survey, 1823

Reading Belief Scales, 6160

Reading Class Attitude Inventory, 544

Reading Comprehension Test, 1055, 1615

Reading Comprehension Tests, 14

Reading Consultant Responsibilities Questionnaire, 1334

Reading-Input Test, 372

Reading Miscue Inventory, 2391

Reading Preference Questionnaire, 1460

Reading Readiness Battery, 1121

Reading Retention Test, 1616

Reading Self-Concept Scale, 6869

Reading Span Test, 2392

Reading-Storage Test, 373

Reading Teacher Survey, Revised Edition, 545

Reading Tests of Flexibility, 15

Reagles Measure of Rehabilitation Gain, 691

Real Estate Career Scale, 2686

Realism of Vocational Plans Scale, 1590

Realistic Expectations Questionnaire, 4935

Realistic Job Expectations Scale, 4936

Realistic Job Preview Scale, 6007

Reasoning about Abortion Questionnaire, 4318

Reasoning Test, 2227

Reasons for Exercise Inventory, 6667

Reasons for Leaving Scale, 6008

Reasons for Living Inventory, 2521, 3917, 5649 [See also Brief Reasons for Living Inventory]

Reasons for Quitting Scale, 4734

Recent Life Changes Questionnaire, 2522

Receptive Language Measure, 2935

Receptivity to Change Scale, 6601

Reciprocal Category System, 1261

Recognition Test, 374

Reconstruction Test, 13

Recreation Experience Preference Scales, 3407

Recreational Therapy Rating Form, 6286

Reduced Behavioral Rehearsal Assertion Test, 3502

Reenlistment Decisions Questionnaire, 3652

Referential Communications Test, 2923

Referral Process Inventory, 2119

Reflections of Self and Environment, 3285

Reflections of Self by Youth, 3286

Reflective Judgment Interview, 5150

Reflective Judgment Scale, 5149, 7140

Reflective Teaching Instrument, 6287

Reformist Dissent Scale, 6009

Regressive Coping Checklist, 5650

Rehabilitation Counseling, Personal Attributes, Work Preferences and Employability Rating Scale, 692

Rehabilitation Services Satisfaction Survey, 182

Reid-Gundlach Social Services Satisfaction Scale, 6602

Reinforcement Inventory, 734

Reinforcement Survey Schedule, 735, 2018

Reinforcing Behaviors of Teachers Questionnaire, 736
Relational Interaction Satisfaction Scale, 5833
Relations and Reality Testing Inventory, 5834
Relationship Assessment Scale, 4058
Relationship Belief Inventory, 3287
Relationship Beliefs Questionnaire, 6870
Relationship Beliefs Scale, 5835
Relationship Events Scale, 2597
Relationship Inventory, 148, 220, 1262, 2353, 3594 [See also Barrett-Lennard Relationship Inventory]
Relationship Judgment Test, 2936
Relationship Questionnaire, 330, 3595 [See also Sorenson Relationship Questionnaire; Truax-Carkhuff Relationship Questionnaire—Short Form]
Relationship Satisfaction Scale, 5836
Relationship Stress Scale, 4059
Relationship with Father Scale, 653
Relationships Influencing Career Planning Scale, 2228
Relative Deprivation Scale, 6010
Relaxation Inventory, 3918
Religion-Science Conflict Scale, 7248
Religiosity Index, 3553
Religiosity Questionnaire, 1525
Religiosity Scale, 2322, 3554, 5241, 7249
Religious Attitude Scale, 1178
Religious Belief Questionnaire, 2323
Religious Commitment Scale, 982
Religious Dogma Scale, 983
Religious Experience Episodes Measure, 2324 [See also Hood Religious Experience Episodes Measure]

Religious Groups Questionnaire, 183
Religious Identification Scale, 5242
Religious Ideology Scale, 7250
Religious Locus of Control Scale, 4937
Religious Orientation Scale, 7251
Religious Orientation Scale— Allport-Ross Version, 5243
Religious Orientation Scale— Revised, 7252
Religious Questionnaire, 984
Religious Relativism Index, 3555
Reminiscence Measures, 812
Remote Associates Test, 132, 2941
Report of Child Behavior, 4438
Representational Systems Inventory, 4938
Repression-Sensitization Scale, 293, 951, 1875, 3503, 3919, 3920 [See also Byrne Repression-Sensitization Scale]
Repression-Sensitization Scale— Short Version, 3504
Repression-Sensitization Tendencies Scale, 1502
Reproductive Knowledge Scale, 1056
Research Article Rating Scale, 693
Residence Counselor Job Performance Rating Form, 1019
Residence Counselor Survey, 1020
Residence-Hall Counselor Evaluation Scale, 2354
Residence Hall Viewpoints Inventory, 546
Resident Assistant Evaluation Form—R, 5296
Resident Assistant Evaluation Form—RD, 5297
Resident Counselor Evaluation Scale, 2355
Resident Evaluation Form, 2356
Resistance to Deviations Test, 952
Respondent's Psychological Participation Scale, 1419

Response Empathy Rating Scale, 3505

Responsibility Questionnaire, 6288

Responsibility Scale, 4060

Restraint Scale, 1876, 4319, 5837

Rest's Test of Moral Comprehension, 3556

Resultant Achievement Motivation Test—Short Form, 2019 [See also Mehrabian Resultant Achievement Motivation Scales]

Retail Store Department Manager Rating Scale, 1560

Retirement Experiences and Planning Scales, 5651

Rettig Behavior Prediction Scale, 1234

Reversals Test, 813

Revised Behavior Problem Checklist, 6289 [See also Behavior-Problem Checklist]

Revised Children's Manifest Anxiety Scale, 3921, 5652, 7196 [See also Children's Manifest…; Manifest Anxiety Scale, Children's Form]

Revised Class Play, 4061 [See also Class Play]

Revised Craig Lipreading Inventory, 5386

Revised-Individual Questionnaire, 5106

Revised Infant Temperament Questionnaire, 5069 [See also Infant Temperament Questionnaire, Revised]

Revised Love/Hate Checklist, 6290 [See also Love/Hate Checklist]

Revised Personal Attribute Inventory, 6871 [See also Personal Attribute Inventory]

Revised Personal Involvement Inventory—Services, 7104 [See also Modified Personal Involvement…; Personal Involvement Inventory]

Revised Scale for Ambiguity Tolerance, 6873 [See also Ambiguity Tolerance Scale; AT-20; Intolerance of Ambiguity …; Scale of Tolerance-Intolerance of Ambiguity; Tolerance for Ambiguity …]

Revised Self-Monitoring Scale, 4062, 6874 [See also Self-Monitoring Scale]

Revised Situational Attitude Scale, 6161 [See also Situational Attitude Scale]

Reward Contingency Scale, 2120

Reward Inequity Scale, 4939

Reward Level Scale, 2598, 3144

Reward Preference Inventory, 261

Reward-Specific Job Satisfaction, 6011

Rewardingness Scale, 3041

Rheingold Social Responsiveness Scale, 1235

Rhody Secondary Reading Attitude Assessment, 1824

RIAS, 4320 [See also Racial Identity Attitude Scale; White Racial Identity Attitude Scale]

Ricks-Epley-Wessman Temporal Experience Questionnaire, 1420

Right Hemisphere Orientation Scale, 2687

Right-Left Discrimination Battery—Form A, 1943

Right-Left Discrimination Tests, 814

Right-Wing Authoritarianism Scale, 7197

Rigidity Questionnaire, 5206

Rigidity Test, 2286 [See also Breskin Rigidity Test]

Rigorous Eating Scale, 4439

Rimon's Brief Depression Scale, 3922

Ringel Test of Oral Form Discrimination, 1421

Risk Scales, 4735

Risk-Taking Inventory, 2776

Riskin-Faunce Family Interaction Scales, 597
Roberts and O'Reilly Organizational Communication Questionnaire, 1901
Robustness Semantic Differential Scale, 3107, 6603
Rod and Frame Test, 815 [See also Gerard Rod and Frame Test]
Roe-Siegelman Parent-Child Relations Questionnaire, 149, 654 [See also Parent-Child Relation Questionnaire—Short Form II]
Rokeach Dogmatism Scale, 294, 953 [See also Dogmatism Scale]
Rokeach Dogmatism Scale—Short Form, 2287, 7198 [See also Dogmatism Scale, Short-Form]
Rokeach Self-Report Scale—Revised, 1526
Rokeach Value Survey, 2325, 2326, 7253
Role Ambiguity Index, 6875
Role Ambiguity Scale, 2525, 3288, 4940, 4941, 6876–6880 [See also Role Conflict and...]
Role Behavior Scale, 6506
Role Category Questionnaire, 3408
Role Clarity Scale, 6881, 6882
Role Conflict and Ambiguity Scale, 2121, 2122, 3290
Role Conflict and Ambiguity Scales, 6883
Role Conflict and Enhancement Scale, 4944
Role Conflict and Role Ambiguity Measure, 2357
Role Conflict Scale, 2526, 3289, 4942, 4943, 5107, 6884–6889
Role Consistency Measure, 1461
Role Construct Repertory Test, 816 [See also Kelly Role Construct Repertory Test]
Role Construct Repertory Test—Grid Form, 2229 [See also Bieri Grid; Kelly's Role Construct Repertory Test, Bieri's Modification of]
Role Construct Repertory Test—Modified, 2230
Role Expectations Scale, 3291
Role Perception Scale, 2123
Role Playing Scale, 4945
Role Problems Scale, 4189
Role Quality Scale, 6507
Role Questionnaire, 3292
Role Scale, 6890
Role Spillover Scale, 6891
Role Strain Scale, 4946, 6012
Role Strain Scales, 6892
Role Stress Scale, 2527
Role-Taking Egocentrism Scale, 1503
Role-Taking Test, 579, 1236 [See also Feffer Role Taking Test]
Role-Type Identification Questionnaire, 331
Rollins Child-Rearing Scale, 3042
Romantic Attitudes Scales, 2777
Romantic Attraction Scale, 5838
Romantic Love Complex Scales, 295
Romantic Love Scale—Korean Version, 5840
Romantic Love Symptom Checklist, 2599, 2600
Romanticism Scale, 5839
Roommate Checklist, 262
Roommate Rapport Scale, 4063
Roommate Rapport Scale—Short Form, 4064
Roos Time Reference Inventory, 91
Rosen Job Environment Questionnaire, 6013
Rosenberg Self Esteem Scale, 817, 2124, 3293, 4948, 4949 [See also Scale of Self-Esteem; Self-Esteem Scale]
Rosenzweig Picture-Frustration Study, 2528 [See also Picture-Frustration Study]

Rotter I-E Scale, 4947, 6893 [See also I-E Locus of Control Scale; I-E Scale]

Rotter Internal-External Locus of Control Scale, 221, 6894 [See also Internal-External Locus of Control Scale]

Rotter Internal-External Scale, 818 [See also Internal-External Scale]

Rotter Interpersonal Trust Scale, 954, 1504, 2288 [See also Interpersonal Trust Scale]

Routinization Scale, 6604

Rudin's Rational Authority Scale, 296

Runner Studies of Attitude Patterns—College Form, 222

Russell Sage Social Relations Test, 456

Rydell-Rosen Tolerance of Ambiguity Scale, 955, 1505

Rystrom Dialect Test, 105

S

S-R Inventory of Anxiousness, Hedquist & Weinhold Revision of, 286

S-R Inventory of General Trait Anxiousness, 3935

S-R Inventory of Hostility, 7050

S-R Inventory of Machiavellianism, 3514

Sage's Developmental Scale, 223

Salary Equity/Satisfaction Scale, 4190

Sales Performance Chart, 3596

Sales Performance Perceptions Scales, 6895

Sales Type A Personality Index—Short Form, 3508

Salespeople Motivation Scale, 6668

Salesperson Trust of Sale Manager Scale, 6014

Salesperson's Job Performance Questionnaire, 5298

Salience and Clarity of Career Strategy Scale, 5348

Salience Assessment Task, 1422

Salivary Response to Lemon Juice Introversion Measure, 956

SAMPLE Profile, 1877, 5841

San Diego Quick Assessment Check, 375

Sapir Developmental Scale-C, 1289

Sarason Test Anxiety Questionnaire, 398 [See also Mandler-Sarason Test Anxiety Questionnaire]

Sarason Test Anxiety Scale, 399 [See also Mandler-Sarason Test Anxiety Scale; Test Anxiety Scale]

Sarbin-Rosenberg Adjective Check List, 819

Sarnoff Survey of Attitudes toward Life, 3145

Satisfaction Opinionnaire, 5349, 7428

Satisfaction Scale, 2659

Satisfaction with College Major Index, 876

Satisfaction with Communication in Dating Relationships Questionnaire, 5842

Satisfaction with Communication Scale, 6354

Satisfaction with Illness Scale, 5653

Satisfaction with Life Scale, 2529, 3923, 3924, 5654

Satisfaction with Material Rewards Scale, 4191

Satisfaction with My Supervisor Scale, 6015

Satisfaction with Parenting Scale, 4617

Satisfaction with Performance Appraisal Scale, 4192

Satisfaction with School Scale, 3727

Satisfaction with the Navy Scale, 2661

Satisfaction with 3/38 Work Schedule Scale, 2660

Scale for Measuring Attitudes toward Any Teacher, 580

Scale for Rating Behavioral Characteristics of Superior Students, 6291 [See also Behavioral Characteristics Rating Scale for Superior Students]

Scale for Suicide Ideation, 3925, 5655 [See also Modified Scale for Suicidal Ideation; Suicide Ideation Scale]

Scale for Suicide Ideators, 2530

Scale of Alienation, 64 [See also Alienation Scale]

Scale of Attitudes toward Change, 92

Scale of Competency in Independent Living Skills, 3926

Scale of Counseling Dimension Preferences, 3409

Scale of General Alienation, 65

Scale of Intellectual Development, 2958, 4515, 6378

Scale of Psychosomatic Symptoms of Stress, 423

Scale of Self-Esteem, 3295 [See also Rosenberg Self Esteem Scale; Self-Esteem Scale]

Scale of Thoughts in Oral Examinations, 5424

Scale of Tolerance-Intolerance of Ambiguity, 3509 [See also Ambiguity Tolerance Scale; AT-20; Intolerance of Ambiguity...; Revised Scale for Ambiguity Tolerance; Tolerance for Ambiguity...]

Scale of Vocational Indecision, 5350

Scale on Use and Value of Guidance Practices, 185

Scale to Assess World Views, 4950

Scale to Assess World Views (Modified), 7254

Scales for Investigation of the Dual-Career Family—Revised, 3043 [See also Dual-Career Family Scale]

Scales of Motivation for College, 208

SCERC Information Test in Rehabilitation Counseling, 1057

SCERC Supervisory Rating Blank, 1561

Schaefer Classroom Behavior Inventory, 1237 [See also Classroom Behavior Inventory; Classroom Behavior Inventory, Preschool to Primary]

Schaefer Parent Behavior Inventory, 655

Schedule for Classroom Activity Norms, 1878

Schedule of Recent Events, 2531

Schedule of Recent Experiences, 1290, 2532, 2533

Schematizing Test, 2289

Schoenfeld Daydreams Inventory, 858

Scholastic Self Concept Scale, 6896

School Acceptance Scale, 1070

School Adjustment Index, 3728

School Adjustment Scale, 3729

School Administrator Morale Measure, 1978

School Administrator Morale Measure: III, 1680

School Attachment Measure, 3730

School Attitude Research Instrument, 66

School Attitude Scale, 1825, 2778

School Behavior Profile, 1238

School Climate Questionnaire, 3108

School Counselor Attitude Inventory, 1826

School Counselors' Checklist, 820

School Drop Out Prediction Scale, 476

School Environment Preference Schedule, 957

School Failure Tolerance Scale, 3731, 5425
School Leadership Inventory, 2872
School Learning Environment Schedule, 3109
School Motivation Scale, 737, 4736, 6669 [See also Phillips School Motivation Scale]
School of Nursing Evaluative Q-Sort, 694
School Organization Inventory, 695
School Organization Scales, 6605
School Organizational Rigidity Scale, 4672
School Orientation Scale, 547
School Participant Empowerment Scale, 6016
School Psychologist Stress Inventory, 2662
School Rating Scale, 548
School-Related Attitudes Scale, 5426
School Related Curiosity Scale, 4673
School Sentiment Index, 1179
School Sentiment Inventory, 2779, 4951
School Situations Picture Stories Test, 738
School Survey, 1827
School Vision Inventory, 4952
Schutz' Fundamental Interpersonal Orientations Test, Form B, 67 [See also Fundamental Interpersonal Relations Orientation...]
Science Activity Questionnaire, 3732
Science Anxiety Questionnaire, 5427
Science Attitude Scales, 4321
Science Cognitive Preference Inventory, 3410
Science Laboratory Environment Inventory, 6606
Science Process Skill Test, 7141
Scientific Orientation Scale, 7105

Scientist-Practitioner Inventory, 7429
SCL-90, 1681 [See also Symptom Checklist-90]
Screening Ability Scale, 5387
Screening Test of Auditory Perceptual Skills, 1423
SD-25, 4487 [See also Self-Disclosure Questionnaire; Self-Disclosure Scale]
Sears' Self-Concept Inventory, 1424 [See also Self-Concept Inventory—Revised]
Seat Belt Attitudes and Beliefs Questionnaire, 1828
Seat Belt Beliefs Scale, 1829
Seat Belt Scales, 2780
Seat Belt Use Questionnaire, 1879
Secondary Student Attitude toward Education Measure, 549
Seeking of Noetic Goals Test (SONG), 821
SEK Test, 5388
Self-Acceptance and Acceptance of Others Form, 1880
Self-Acceptance and Acceptance of Others Scale, 4065
Self-Acceptance Scale, 1425, 2125, 3296
Self-Actualization Scale, 4953
Self-Aggression Scale, 242
Self-Anchoring Striving Scale, 2020 [See also Cantril's Self-Anchoring Striving Scale]
Self and Ideal Self Q Sort, 822
Self and Prestige Scale, 2239
Self-Appraisal Inventory—School Relations, 4954
Self-Appraisal of Curiosity Inventory, 2021
Self as Counselor, Ideal Counselor, Other Counselor, Semantic Differential Instrument, 1426
Self-Assessment of Relative Strengths in Teaching, 5299
Self-Assessment Questionnaire, 3653

Self-Assessment Questionnaire—
Nijmegen, 5656
Self-Assurance Scale, 1427
Self-Care Inventory, 4440
Self-Cathexis Scale, 2126, 4955
Self-Concealment Scale, 6292
Self-Concept and Motivation
Inventory (SCAMIN), 3297
Self-Concept Appraisal Scales, 3298
Self-Concept as a Learner Scale,
3299
Self-Concept Inventory, 2127
Self-Concept Inventory, Alternate
Form, 2035
Self-Concept Inventory—Revised,
243, 4956 [See also Sears' Self-
Concept Inventory]
Self-Concept Measure, 3300
Self-Concept/Occupational Concept
Distance Scale, 3654
Self-Concept of Ability Instrument,
1428
Self Concept of Ability Question-
naire, 1429
Self-Concept of Ability—Revised,
823
Self-Concept of Ability Scale, 3301
[See also Brookover's Self-
Concept of Ability Scale]
Self-Concept of Academic Ability
Scale, 2128, 6897
Self-Concept Scale, 4957
Self-Concept Semantic Differential,
1430, 2129
Self-Concept Semantic Differential
Rating Scale, 2130
Self-Consciousness Scale, 3302,
3376, 4958–4961, 5070, 6898,
7041, 7042
Self-Consciousness Scale—Brazil-
ian Version, 7043
Self-Consciousness Scale—Italian
Version, 6899
Self-Consciousness Scale—Revised,
4962, 7040
Self-Consciousness Scale, Social
Anxiety Subscale, 2605

Self-Consciousness Scale (Spanish),
3927
Self-Control Questionnaire, 4963
Self-Control Rating Scale, 6293
Self-Control Schedule, 2873, 4441,
5207, 6294, 7044
Self-Critical Cognition Scale, 6901
Self-Criticism Scale, 244
Self-Deception and Impression
Management Scales, 5071
Self-Deception and Other-Deception
Questionnaires, 6902
Self-Deception Questionnaire, 3510
Self-Defeating Personality Scale,
5072, 7045
Self-Derogation Scale, 2131
Self-Description Blank, 6379
Self-Description Inventory, 6903,
6904 [See also Ghiselli Self-
Description Inventory]
Self-Description Inventory—
Revised, 4066
Self-Description Questionnaire,
245, 3303, 3304
Self-Description Questionnaire III,
3305, 4964, 4965
Self-Descriptive Inventory for
African Adolescents, 6905
Self-Descriptive List, 2132
Self-Descriptive Q-Set, 6906
Self-Descriptive Questionnaire,
2022
Self-Directed Learning Readiness
Scale, 2193
Self-Directed Learning Readiness
Scale—Abbreviated Form, 1742
Self-Disclosure Inventory, 1902
Self-Disclosure Inventory for
Adolescents—Revised, 4488
Self-Disclosure Measure, 1263
Self-Disclosure Questionnaire, 104,
1264, 1265 [See also Jourard Self
Disclosure Questionnaire; SD-25]
Self Disclosure Questionnaire—
Adapted, 598

Self-Disclosure Scale, 4489 [See also Jourard's Self-Disclosure Scale; SD-25]
Self-Disclosure Scales, 6355
Self-Disclosure Sentence Completion Blank, 4490
Self-Discrimination Semantic Differential Instrument, 1431
Self-Dyadic Perspective-Taking Scale, 4067
Self-Efficacy Expectations Scale, 6907
Self-Efficacy for Computer Technologies, 6908
Self-Efficacy for Technical/Scientific Fields Scale, 3733
Self-Efficacy for Work Activities Scale, 6909
Self-Efficacy/Interest Rating Scale, 4966, 5108
Self-Efficacy Inventory, 4967, 4968
Self-Efficacy Measures, 3306
Self-Efficacy Questionnaire, 4969, 6910
Self-Efficacy Scale, 3307, 3308, 4970, 4972, 6911–6916
Self-Efficacy Scale—Revised, 4971
Self-Efficacy toward Teaching Inventory, 6917
Self-Empowerment Index, 6918
Self-Esteem Inventory, 2133, 2137, 3309, 4973, 6919 [See also Coopersmith Self-Esteem Inventory]
Self-Esteem Inventory—Form B, 3310
Self-Esteem Inventory—General Self Subscale, 3311
Self-Esteem Inventory—Revised, 824
Self-Esteem Measure, 2134
Self-Esteem Questionnaire, 2135, 4974
Self-Esteem Rating Scale for Children, 4975

Self-Esteem Scale, 246, 825–827, 2136, 2138, 2139, 3312–3315, 4976–4978, 6920–6927 [See also Rosenberg Self Esteem Scale; Scale of Self-Esteem]
Self-Esteem Scales, 2140
Self-Estimate Questionnaire, 1591
Self-Estrangement Scale, 457
Self-Evaluated Intelligence Scale, 247
Self-Evaluated Sales Performance Measure, 3598
Self-Evaluation of Communication Experiences after Laryngectomy Scale, 6356
Self Evaluation of Life Function Scale, 3928
Self Evaluation Questionnaire, 828
Self-Evaluative Inventory, 2141
Self-Expectations Instrument, 1432
Self-Expression Inventory, 4442, 6928
Self-Focus Sentence Completion, 5208, 7046 [See also Exner Self Focus Sentence Completion]
Self-Handicapping Scale, 6295–6297
Self-Image Disparity Questionnaire, 4979
Self-Image Questionnaire, 4980
Self-Image Questionnaire for Young Adolescents, 4981
Self-Image Scale, 6929
Self-Liking/Self-Competence Scale, 6930
Self-Management Practices Scale, 6298, 6299
Self-Mastery Scale, 6931
Self-Monitoring Scale, 3686, 4068, 4982, 4983, 6932, 6933 [See also Revised Self-Monitoring Scale]
Self-Motivation Inventory, 4737, 6670
Self-Others Scales, 5843
Self-Peer Need Rating, 1359
Self-Perceived Popularity Measure, 458

Self-Perception Index, 829
Self-Perception of Attainment
    Scale, 5011
Self-Perception Profile for Adoles-
    cents, Global Self-Worth
    Subscale, 6760
Self-Perception Profile for Adoles-
    cents—Norwegian Version, 6934
Self-Perception Profile for Children,
    6935
Self-Perception Test, 6936
Self-Rated Competence, 2924
Self-Rating Anxiety Scale, 1682,
    3929
Self-Rating Depression Inventory,
    2142
Self-Rating Depression Scale, 3930,
    5657, 5658 [See also Zung Self-
    Rating Depression Scale]
Self-Rating Scale, 248, 550, 5659
Self-Regulation Scale, 6300, 6301,
    6937
Self-Regulatory Style Question-
    naire, 4738
Self-Report Absence Measure, 6302,
    6303
Self-Report Delinquency Scale,
    2874
Self-Report Family Inventory, 6508
Self-Report Handedness Inventory,
    7106
Self-Report Health Scale, 5661
Self Report Inventory, 551
Self-Report Measure of Conformity,
    2290
Self-Report Measure of Food
    Consumption, 4444
Self-Report Psychopathy Scale,
    3511
Self-Report Questionnaire, 1631
Self-Report Reinforcement Instru-
    ment, 739
Self-Report Trust Scale, 958, 4069
Self-Reported Early Delinquency
    Instrument, 4443

Self-Reported Rating Inflation
    Measure, 6938
Self-Reported Self-Appraisal Scale,
    4984
Self-Reported Symptom Survey,
    5660
Self-Righteousness Scale, 3512,
    5209
Self-Social Constructs Scale, 830
Self-Social Symbols Task, 249
Self-Social Symbols Tasks, 1728
Self-Sort-Ideal-Sort Discrepancy
    Score, 831
Self-Statement Inventory, 6939
Self-Talk Scale, 6304
Self-Uncertainty Scale, 5351
Self- versus Other-Centered Values
    Scale, 2327
Selfism Scale, 3316
Selling Orientation Customer
    Measure, 7320
Sells and Roff Scale of Peer Rela-
    tions, 2601
Selltiz Expectations about College
    Performance Questionnaire, 740
Semantic Consensus Index (SCI),
    1276
Semantic Differential, 1180, 1181
    [See also Myrick Semantic
    Differential]
Semantic Differential—Creativity,
    614
Semantic Differential for Secondary
    School Students, 93
Semantic Differential Instrument,
    121
Semantic Differential Personality
    Measure, 1451
Semantic Differential Scales, 68
Semantic Differential Schedule, 250
Semantic Differential Tempera-
    ment Scales, 2291
Sensation Seeking Scale, 741, 2023,
    2024, 2172, 3146, 6671 [See also
    Impulsivity and Sensation
    Seeking Scales]

Sensation Seeking Scale for Children, 6672
Sensation Seeking Scale—Form V, 6673
Sensation Seeking Scale, Form VI, 3147
Sensation-Seeking Scale IV, 2025
Sensation-Seeking Scale (Short Form), 4739
Sense of Autonomy Scale, 4445
Sense of Coherence Scale, 3931, 4985, 6940
Sense of Community Index—Short Form, 4674
Sense of Community Scale—City Subscale, 5844
Sense of Competence and Time-Dimension Scale, 4989
Sense of Competence Measure, 3317
Sense of Competence Question-naire, 4987
Sense of Competence Scale, 4986, 4988, 6941
Sense of Control Scale, 6942, 6943
Sense of Humor Questionnaire, 5662
Sensitivity to Rejection Scale, 69, 1726
Sentence Completion Question-naire, 1830
Sentence Completion Scale, 3148
Sentence Completion Test, 122, 1944, 2959, 4516 [See also Washington University Sentence Completion Test]
Sentence Completion Test of Achievement Motivation, 2026
Sentence Completion Test of Safety and Esteem Motives, 1360
Sentence Completion Test—Shortened Form, 4517 [See also Washington University Sentence Completion Test—Short Form]
Sentence-Imitation Test, 376, 377
Sentence Selection Test, 2231
Sentences Completion Test, 5663

Separation Anxiety Test, 3932
Separation-Individuation Inven-tory, 4070, 6380
Separation-Individuation Test of Adolescence, 6509
Series Learning Potential Test, 1743
Serious Theft Scale, 6162
Seriousness of Illness Scale, 5664
Service Orientation Index for Nurses Aides, 3377
SERVQUAL, 6607
Session Evaluation Questionnaire, 3599, 5300, 7321–7324
Session Evaluation Questionnaire—Form 2, 5301
Session Evaluation Questionnaire—Form 4, 7325
Session Impacts Scale, 7326
Seven-Level Occupational Status Scale, 276
Seven Secrets Survey Retrospective, 6510
Sex-Based Equal Opportunity Scale, 4675
Sex History Questionnaire, 4446
Sex Information Questionnaire, 2393
Sex Knowledge and Attitude Test, 2781, 3687
Sex Role Achievement Standards Measure, 877
Sex-Role Antecedents Scales, 5109
Sex-Role Attitude Scale, 1831
Sex Role Attitudes Scale, 6164, 7107
Sex Role Behavior Scale, 5110
Sex Role Behavior Scale—Short Form, 5111
Sex Role Career Indecision Scale for Women, 7108
Sex-Role Conflict Scale, 4193, 5112
Sex Role Disapproval Measure, 2194
Sex-Role Egalitarianism Scale, 2782, 7109

Sex-Role Egalitarianism Scale
    (Short Form), 4322
Sex-Role Ideology Scale, 3411, 5113,
    7110
Sex Role Learning Index, 2195
Sex-Role Orientation Scale, 2783,
    5114
Sex Role Questionnaire, 552, 2196
Sex Role Rating Questionnaire, 878
Sex Role Scale, 7111
Sex Stereotype Measure (Korean),
    3318
Sex Stereotype Questionnaire, 3319
Sexes: An Attitude Inventory, 1834
Sexist Attitudes toward Women
    Scale, 6163
Sexual Abuse Scale, 4447
Sexual Arousability Index, 4448
Sexual Attitude Scale, 4323
Sexual Desire Conflict Scale for
    Women, 5665
Sexual Experience Scale, 4449
Sexual Experience Survey, 6307
Sexual Experiences Questionnaire,
    4676, 6305, 6306
Sexual Experiences Survey, 2875
Sexual Fantasy Questionnaire,
    2876
Sexual Intentions Scale, 6674
Sexual Permissiveness Scale, 6165,
    6308
Sexual Response Cycle, 4740
Sexual Sensation-Seeking Scale,
    6675
Sexual Sensation Seeking Scale,
    Revised, 6676
Sexual Socialization Scale, 5845
Sexuality Scales, 5666
Sexually Harassing Behaviors
    Scale, 6309
SF Test, 2293 [See also F-Scale]
Shalling Sifneos Personality Scale,
    5073
Shame-Proneness Questionnaire,
    5667
Shape-O Ball Test, 477, 2143

Shared Activities Questionnaire,
    6511
Shared Personal Constructs, 1305
Sherman-Kulhavy Laterality
    Assessment Inventory, 1881
Shigaki-Wolf Logic Test, 3441
Shimkunas Uncertainty Anxiety
    Scale, 960
Shop and Laboratory Inventory,
    1182
Shopping Involvement Scale, 7112
Shopping Orientation Scale, 4450
Shopping Orientation Scales, 7113
Short Balanced F Scale, 7199 [See
    also F Scale, Balanced (Short
    Form)]
Short Index of Self-Actualization,
    4990, 6944, 6945
Short Marital Adjustment Test,
    4618 [See also Locke Wallace
    Short Marital Adjustment Test]
Short-Term Memory Test, 18
"Show Me" Test, 1183
Shyness Response Scale, 5210
Shyness Scale, 5211, 7201
Shyness Scale (Cheek and Buss),
    Revised, 5205
Sibling Relationship Inventory,
    6512
Sibling Relationship Questionnaire,
    3044
Sibling Relationships Question-
    naire, 4619
Sick Role Questionnaire, 1239
Sight Word Vocabulary Test, 2937
Significance Scale, 696
Silencing the Self Scale, 6310
Simile Appreciation Scale, 2938
Similes Preference Inventory, 959
    [See also Pearson-Maddi Similes
    Preference Inventory—Revised]
Simon-Dole Listening Comprehen-
    sion Test, 2688
Simulated Social Interaction Test,
    2602
Simulation of Interactive Decision
    Making, Version 1, 7327

Simulation of Interactive Decision Making—Version 2, 7328
Sinha Self Disclosure Inventory, 599
Situational Attitude Scale, 6166 [See also Revised Situational Attitude Scale]
Situational Attitude Scale—Handicapped, 2784
Situational Case Questionnaire to Assess Damaging Information on Application, 553
Situational Characteristics Questionnaire, 5668
Situational Constraints Scale, 6017
Situational Guilt Scale, 5074
Situational Humor Response Questionnaire, 3933, 5669
Situational Inventory of Body-Image Dysphoria, 6946
Situational Response Test, 1462
Situations Inventory, 1683
Six-Factor Self-Concept Scale, 6947
Skill Development Scale, 6381, 6382
Skill Utilization Inventory, 6019
Skills and Abilities Confidence Scale, 6018
Skills Rating Inventory, 3320
Skin Color Preference, 1463
Skinner's Radical Behaviorism Test, 5389
Slang Test, 378, 1058
Slater Nursing Competence Rating Scale, 3597
Sleep Questionnaire, 2877
Smith Impulsivity-Constricted Scale, 961
Smith Test for Measuring Teacher Judgment of Written Composition, 1031, 1059
Smoking Specific Locus of Control Scale, 6948
Social Access Questionnaire, 1452
Social Activities Scale, 5846
Social Activity Measure, 5847
Social Activity Questionnaire, 2603

Social Adjustment and Employment Scales, 4071
Social and Existential Courage Scale, 1832
Social Anhedonia Scale, 5848
Social Anomia Scale, 2612
Social Anxiety Index for Anxiety, 4072
Social Anxiety Index for Skill, 4074
Social Anxiety Questionnaire, 4073
Social Anxiety Scale, 2604
Social Anxiety Scale for Children, 4075
Social Assessment Scale—Self-Report, 5849
Social Attitude Q Sort, 554
Social Attitude Referents Scale, 555
Social Attitude Scale, 1527
Social Attitudes Scale, 94
Social Avoidance and Distress Scale, 4076
Social Behavior Assessment—Revised—Teacher Rating Scale, 4077
Social Behavior Inventory—Revised, 3412
Social Behavior Rating Scale, 4078
Social Competence Observation Measure, 2606
Social Competence Scale, 459
Social Coping Questionnaire for Gifted Students, 5670
Social Desirability Questionnaire, 251
Social Desirability Scale, 5850, 5851 [See also Crowne-Marlowe Social Desirability Scale; Marlowe-Crowne Social Desirability Scale]
Social Desirability Scale—Brief Version, 4079
Social Desirability Scale, Revised, 62, 5852
Social Diffusion Questionnaire, 460
Social Distance Index, 1184
Social Distance Questionnaire, 1185

Social Distance Scale, Revised, 63
[See also Bogardus Social
Distance Scale—Modified]
Social Distance Scales toward Male
and Female Homosexuals, 4080
Social Dominance Scale, 5853, 5854
Social Egocentrism Instrument,
1109
Social Functioning Index, 2607
Social Identity Survey, 4991
Social Insight Scale, 5855
Social Integration Scale, 3734, 5856
Social Interaction Scale, 4082
Social Interaction Self-Statement
Test, 4081, 5857
Social Interdependence Scale, 2785
Social Intimacy Scale, 5858 [See
also Miller Social Intimacy Scale]
Social Isolation Scale, 1110, 4083
Social Isolation Scale—Modified,
1727
Social Order Scale, 3557
Social-Organizational Question-
naire, 1979
Social Orientation Inventory, 4741
Social Performance Survey Sched-
ule, 2608, 2609
Social Performance Survey Sched-
ule—Revised, 2610
Social, Personality, and Demo-
graphic Questionnaire, 2173
Social Phobia and Anxiety Inven-
tory, 7047
Social-Political Future Time
Perspective, 832
Social Power Questionnaire, 1112
Social Problem-Solving Inventory
for Adolescents, 5860
Social Propensity Scale, 2611
Social Provisions Scale, 4084, 5861
Social Provisions Scale—Modified,
4085
Social Reaction Inventory, 4992
Social Reactions Inventory, 5862
Social Readjustment Rating Scale—
Stressful Life Events, 2423

Social Reflection Measure—Short
Form, 7255
Social Reinforcement Orientation
Checklist, 2925
Social Relations Survey, 5863
Social-Religious-Political Scale,
4324
Social Responsibility Scale, 1113
Social Reticence Scale, 3513, 7202
Social Roles Instrument, 461
Social Scale, 4325, 6167
Social Scenarios Scale, 4451, 5864
Social Sciences Piagetian Inventory,
2960
Social Skills Checklist, 4086
Social Skills Rating Scale for
Teachers, 4087
Social Skills Survey—Peer, 4088
Social Studies Implications Test,
1282
Social Studies Information Test,
1060
Social Studies Strategies Survey,
5151
Social Support Appraisals Scale,
4620, 5865
Social Support Appraisals Scale—
Revised, 5866
Social Support Behavior Scale, 5867
Social Support from Family Inven-
tory, 4621
Social Support in Response to
Depression Scale, 5869
Social Support Index, 5868
Social Support Inventory, 4089,
5870
Social Support Measure, 5871
Social Support Questionnaire, 5872,
5873
Social Support Questionnaire—
Short Report, 5874
Social Support Scale, 4090–4092,
4622, 4623, 5875, 5876
Social Support Scale for Chinese
Students in Japan, 5877
Social Support Scale for Friends,
4093

Social System Scale, 5878
Social Values Test, 1528
Social Vocabulary Index, 252
Social Welfare Concern Scale, 462
Socialization Scale, 1111
Socially Desirable Response Set-5, 4094, 5859
Socially Responsible Consumer Behavior Scale, 6311
Socioemotional Adjustment Questionnaire, 4095
Socioemotional Support Inventory, 4624
Sociological Journal Evaluative Questionnaire, 906
Sociometric Device, Expanded, 214, 849
Sociometric Peer-Rating Scale, 3449
Sociometric Test, 70
Sociomoral Reflection Measure, 3558
Sociomoral Reflection Objective Measure (Short Form), 4518
Socio-Political Attitudes Scales, 6168
Sociotropy-Autonomy Scale, 7048, 7049
Somatic Complaints Index, 5671
Somatic Complaints Inventory, 5672
Somatic Complaints Scale, 3934, 4194, 4195
Somatic Response Survey, 4452, 5673
Somatic Tension Scale, 5674
"Something about Myself" Check List, 615
Sorenson Relationship Questionnaire, 4993 [See also Relationship Questionnaire]
Source Credibility Manipulation Scale, 6357
Sources of Math Efficacy Scale, 6949
South African Life Event Scale, 3111

Spanish Visual Discrimination Test, 2394
Spatial Activities Questionnaire, 4453
Spatial Dimensionality Test, 4994
Spatial Orientation of Objects Motion Picture Test, 1433
Spatial Test, 1061
Special Incomplete Sentence Tests, 400
Specialty Indecision Scale, 3655
Specific Curiosity Questionnaire, 742
Specific Fear Index, 253
Specific Value Scale, 1529
Speed and Persistence Test, 1361
Speed of Thinking Test, 7142
Spelling Measure, 6363
Spelling-Sound Translation Test, 1062
Spheres of Control Scale, 4096
Sport Competition Anxiety Test, 5212
Sport Interest Inventory, 5879
Sport Socialization Inventory—Spanish Version, 6312
Sports Orientation Questionnaire, 6313, 7430
Spouse Adjective Test, 3045
Spouse Specific Aggression Scale, 4625
Spouse Support Scale, 6513
Springs Task, 2232
Squires Empathy Test, 254
Srole Anomia Scale, 424, 1685 [See also Anomia Scale, Enlarged]
Srole Anomie Scale, 1684 [See also Anomie Scale]
Stability of Self-Scale, 2145
Stable Dispositions Concept Measure, 4454
Staff Development Evaluation Questionnaire, 3112
Staff Development Questionnaire, 3113
Staff-Student Opinion Questionnaire, 186

Stage of Change Scale, 7329
Stages of Concern Questionnaire, 4196
Stages of Concern Questionnaires, 6020
Standard Helpee Stimulus Expressions and Alternate Responses, 38
Standardized Assault Interview, 6314
Stanford Parent Questionnaire, 463
Stanford Preschool I-E Scale, 2146
Stanton Survey, 4455
Starkweather Form Boards Test, 616
Starkweather Originality Test, 617
Starkweather Target Game, 618
State Guidance Office Function Questionnaire, 697
State Self-Esteem Scale, 6950
State Sport-Confidence Inventory, 5075, 6951
State Test Anxiety Report, 5428
State-Trait Anger Scale—Trait, 5213
Statistical Knowledge Test, 5390
Statistics Anxiety Scale, 5429
Statistics Attitude Scale, 6169
Statistics Attitude Survey, 2786, 4326
Status Concern Scale, 5162 [See also Kaufman's Scale of Status Concern]
Status Deference Scale, 5163
Stein Physiognomic Cue Test, 1506
Stepfamily and Stepfather Cognition Scales, 6514
Stephens-Delys Reinforcement Contingency Interview, 1434
Stereotype Measure, 1186
Stereotype Rating Scale, 6952
Stereotype Survey, 2787
Stereotyped Attitude Scale, 4327
Stern's College Characteristics Index, 187 [See also College Characteristic Index]
Stigma Scale, 6315

Stoicism Scale, 7051
Stony Brook Scale, 2878
Store Management Fairness, 6608
Storm and Stress Scale, 6515
Strain Measure, 1686
Strain Scale, 5430, 5675
Strange Situation Behavior Instrument—Revised, 1957
Stranger Role Scale, 4097
Strategies Scale, 5152
Streckler Attitude toward Negro Scale, 1187
Street Gestalt Completion Test, 1617
Strength of Religious Beliefs Scales, 5244
Strength of Will Scale, 6677
Stress Adjective Checklist, 3936
Stress Assessment Package, 2535
Stress at Work Scale, 4197
Stress Diagnostic Survey, 4198
Stress in Medical School Scale (SIMS), 2425
Stress Intensity Scale, 4199
Stress Measure, 1687
Stress Questionnaire, 5678
Stress Reaction Scale, 5679
Stress Reactions Checklist, 5680
Stress-Related Symptoms Checklist, 5681
Stress Response Scale, 2536
Stress Scale, 2537, 5682, 5683
Stress-Symptom Rating Form, 3938
Stress Symptoms Scale, 3939, 3940
Stressful Events/Appraisal Form, 7256
Stressful Life Event Scale, 2424
Stressful Transaction Scale, 5676
Stressor and Coping Response Inventories for Children, 4995
Stressors Inventory, 5677
Stressors of Clergy Children and Couples Scale, 6516
Stressors of Clergy Children Inventory, 3937
Strictness/Supervision Scale, 6517
Strodtbeck Fatalism Scale, 985

Strodtbeck Planfulness Scale, 986
Strodtbeck Thoughtfulness Scale, 987
Stroop Color and Word Test—Group Form, 1934
Structural Analysis of Social Behavior Questionnaires, 4098
Structural Centralization Scale, 4677
Structural Family Interaction Scale—Revised, 4627, 6518
Structural Family System Ratings, 4628
Structure, Climate and Mentoring Scales, 7330
Structure of Intellect Tests, 74
Structure Rating Scale, 4456
Structured Objective Rorschach Test, 224
Structured Situational Test, 656
Student Activist Scale, 2879
Student Adaptation to College Questionnaire, 3735, 5431
Student Adjustment Questionnaire, 5432
Student Alcohol Questionnaire, 6316
Student Aspiration Scale, 2027
Student-Athlete Recruitment Decision-Making Survey, 3413
Student Attitude Inventory, 2028, 6170
Student Attitude Questionnaire, 1188
Student Attitude Scale—Revised, 1530
Student Attitudes and Beliefs Questionnaire, 556
Student Attitudes toward War Scale, 6171
Student Behavior Checklist, 3941
Student Behavior Observation Instrument, 1240, 2880
Student Behaviors Questionnaire, 2881
Student Counselor Rating Scale, 1021

Student Course Evaluation Questionnaire, 698
Student Development Inventory, 2788
Student Drinking Information Scale—Adapted, 4457
Student Evaluation Form, 1562
Student Evaluation of Instruction Questionnaire, 2358
Student Evaluation of Teaching, 3600
Student Evaluation Questionnaire, 1563, 1564
Student Fees and Services Questionnaire, 2789
Student Information Blank, 225
Student Jenkins Activity Survey, 7203
Student Learning and Motivation Scales, 6678
Student Learning Environment Questionnaire, 3114
Student Motivation and Attitudes Questionnaire, 743
Student Observation Form, 2882
Student Opinion Poll II, 1071
Student-Opinion Questionnaire, 1022, 1565 [See also Bryan's Student Opinion Questionnaire—Revised]
Student Opinion Scale, 95
Student Orientation Survey, 879
Student Participation Questionnaire, 6317
Student Perception of Academic Climate, 1335
Student Perception Scales, 3322
Student Perceptions of the Value of Mathematics Scales, 5245
Student Performance Attribution Scale, 3323
Student Personnel Inventory, 859
Student Preference Schedule, 263
Student Problem Areas Survey, 1980
Student Product Assessment Form, 6370

Student Questionnaire, 1189
Student Rating of Counseling Interview Questionnaire, 699
Student Ratings of Teachers Scale, 3601
Student Religiosity Questionnaire, 7257
Student Resistance to Schooling Inventory, 5433
Student Satisfaction Scale, 5434
Student Self-Concept Scale, 3321
Student Sexual Attitude Scale, 4328
Student Social Orientations Questionnaire, 4329
Student Social Worker Semantic Differential, 1277
Student Stress Inventory, 5437
Student Support and Role Congruence Questionnaire, 2426
Student Survey of School Situations, 700
Student Teacher Concerns Rating Scale, 701
Student Teacher Rating Scale, 3602
Student-Teacher Relationship Scale, 6953
Student Teaching Rating Form, 5302
Student Worry Survey, 3737
Students' Attitudes toward Women's Increased Participation in Social, Economic, and Political Spheres Questionnaire, 1190
Students Conflict Stress Scale, 5435
Students' Evaluations of Educational Quality, 7331
Students' Events Stress Scale, 5436
Students' Life Satisfaction Scale, 5684
Student's Perception of Ability Scale, 2147, 3736
Study Habits and Interest Inventory, 3738
Study Management and Academic Results Test, 6059
Study Process Questionnaire, 5153

Study Process Questionnaire— Arabic Version, 7143
Study Skills Questionnaire, 2883
Study Strategy Questionnaire, 1072
Study Techniques Questionnaire, 1073
Styles of Categorization Test, 1464
Subjective Career Success, 6021
Subjective Expectancies Inventory, 4996
Subjective Marital Dependency Scale, 3046
Subjective Social Support Scale, 4099
Subjective Stress Scale, 833, 1086, 4200
Subjective Underemployment Scale, 6022
Subjective Unit of Discomfort Indicator, 5685
Subjectivism Scale, 5076
Subjects Uses Test, 1911
Subordinate Influence Tactics Scale, 4458
Subordinate Perceptions Scale, 3324
Subordinate-Supervisor Trust, 6023
Subordinate's Confidence in Appraisal, 6609
Substance Abuse Attitude Survey, 4330
Substance Abuse Scales, 1191
Substance-Use Scale, 2790, 4459
Substitutes for Leadership Questionnaire, 4460
Substitutes for Leadership Scale— Revised, 6318, 6319
Substitutes for Leadership Scales, 4678
Success Avoidance Measure, 1362
Success-Failure Inventory, 1833 [See also McReynolds Success Failure Inventory]
Successive Figures Motion Picture Test, 1435
Suicidal Intent Scale, 1688

Suicidal Tendencies Testing Procedure, 2538
Suicide Contemplation Measure, 1087
Suicide Ideation Scale, 3942 [See also Modified Scale for Suicidal Ideation; Scale for Suicide Ideation]
Suicide Questionnaire, 1088
Suicide Semantic Differential, 1192
Suinn-Lew Asian Self-Identity Acculturation Scale, 4100, 5880
Suinn Test Anxiety Behavior Scale, 1074, 2427, 3739
Sundberg Test of Implied Meaning, 1278
Super Neuroticism Scale, 39
Superficial Engagement Scale, 7144
Superiority Scale, 4519, 4742, 6954, 7204
Supernaturalism Questionnaire, 4997
Supervisee Levels Questionnaire, 3325
Supervising Petty Officer Questionnaire, 7332
Supervision Level Scale, 4679
Supervision Questionnaire, 188
Supervisor Attitudes and Behavior Scale, 6172
Supervisor Evaluation Ratings, 7333
Supervisor Fairness Scale, 6955
Supervisor Support Scale, 6024, 7334, 7335
Supervisor's Application of Discipline Scale, 3326
Supervisory Behavior Description Questionnaire, 1241
Supervisory Performance Rating Instrument, 1023
Supervisory Rating Form, 1566
Supervisory Styles Inventory, 3603, 4461, 7336
Support Scale, 5881
Supportive Leadership Behavior Scale, 2884

Supportive Leadership Scale, 6320
Supportive Parenting Scale, 6519
Suppression Scale, 3943
Surface Development Test, 2144
Survey for Writing Attitudes, 6173
Survey of Achievement Responsibility, 4998
Survey of Attitude, 1193 [See also Attitude Survey]
Survey of Attitudes, 1194
Survey of Attitudes toward Statistics, 6174 [See also Attitudes toward Statistics]
Survey of Career Plans and Experiences, 202
Survey of Classroom Behavior, 581
Survey of Eating Patterns, 4462
Survey of Employee Opinions, 1592
Survey of Feelings about Tests, 2428
Survey of Heterosexual Interactions, 2885, 4101
Survey of Heterosocial Interactions for Females, 4102
Survey of Organizations, 6610
Survey of Perceived Organizational Support, 4680, 4681, 6611
Survey of Perceived Supervisory Support, 4682
Survey of Personal Beliefs, 5154
Survey of Student Counseling Needs, 4999
Survey of Student Needs, 5438
Survey of Student Opinion of Teaching, 1024
Survey of Study Habits and Attitudes, Modification of, 23
Survey of Work Values, 1531, 1532, 2328
Survey of Work Values—Modified, 3559
Sustaining Fantasy Questionnaire—Short Form, 2886
Swedish Six-Month Temperament Questionnaire, 3378
Swedish Temperament Questionnaire, 3379

Sydney Attribution Scale, 3327, 5000, 5439
Symbol Identities Test, 1618
Symbols Test, 1744
Symptom Attribution Question-naire, 6956
Symptom Check List, 1632
Symptom Checklist, 425, 1689, 5686
Symptom Checklist-10, 3945
Symptom Checklist-90, 2539, 3944 [See also SCL-90]
Symptom Checklist-90—Revised, 5687
Symptom Questionnaire, 4463
Symptom Survey, 3947, 3948
Symptoms of Stress Inventory, 3946, 5688
Synonyms Test, 1912
Syracuse Scales of Social Rela-tions—Revised, 464

T

Tactics of Influence Scale, 4201
Tactics Scale, 1882
Tagatz Information Processing Test, 605
"Tall Poppy" Scale, 6175
Taped Notetaking Test, 379
Target Complaints Scale, 5689
Task and Ego Orientation in Sport Questionnaire, 7052
Task Arousal Scale, 3149
Task Autonomy Scale, 6612
Task Characteristics Question-naire—Modified, 1981
Task Complexity Scale, 3115
Task Difficulty Questionnaire, 6025
Task Leadership Identity Scale, 6957
Task Leadership Performance Scale, 6321
Task Satisfaction Scale, 2663, 4202

Task-Specific and Social Self-Esteem Scales, 3328
Task-Specific Self-Efficacy Scale, 6958
Task-Specific Self-Esteem Scale, 3329
Taxonomy of Problematic Social Situations for Children, 2613
Taylor Manifest Anxiety Scale, 860, 7205 [See also Manifest Anxiety Scale]
Teacher-Administrator Question-naire, 1195
Teacher Assessment of Students Scale, 3116
Teacher Attitude Instrument, 1196
Teacher Attitude Questionnaire, 557
Teacher Attitude Scale, 4331
Teacher Attitude toward Counsel-ing and Guidance, 189
Teacher Attitude toward Gifted Children Instrument, 558
Teacher Attitudes about Research Questionnaire, 6176
Teacher Behavior Scale, 2887
Teacher Behaviors Inventory, 3605
Teacher Behaviors Questionnaire, 4332
Teacher Belief Inventory, 7258
Teacher Beliefs about Instructional Media, 6177
Teacher Burnout Scale, 4203, 4204
Teacher Burnout Survey, 2664
Teacher Checklist, 6322
Teacher-Child Rating Scale, 3740, 4464, 6323
Teacher-Classroom Adjustment Rating Scale, 3741
Teacher Classroom Behavior Scale, 2888
Teacher Commitment and Job Scales, 5352
Teacher Competence Rating Scales, 1025
Teacher Competency Scale, 1567

Teacher Concerns Questionnaire, 4205

Teacher Education Program Evaluation Scale—Revised, 1982

Teacher Effectance Motivation Rating, 3150

Teacher Effectiveness Questionnaire, 1568

Teacher Effectiveness Scale, 7337

Teacher Effectiveness Survey, 7338

Teacher Efficacy and Control Scales, 6026

Teacher Efficacy Scale, 3331, 5001–5004, 6959–6961

Teacher Image Questionnaire, 1026

Teacher Inventory of Program Standards, 6962

Teacher Leadership Behavior Scale, 2889

Teacher Leadership Style Scale, 1507

Teacher Locus of Control Scale, 3332–3334, 5005, 6963

Teacher Loyalty Questionnaire, 1883

Teacher Observation Form, 7339

Teacher Observation of Classroom Adaption, 6324

Teacher Occupational Stress Factor Questionnaire, 2665, 3117, 4206

Teacher Participation Scale, 4465

Teacher Perceptions of Parent and Teacher Efficacy, 6965

Teacher Perceptions of Teacher Efficacy Scale, 6964

Teacher Performance Evaluation Scale, 1027

Teacher Preference for Classroom Management Strategy, 880

Teacher-Pupil Question Inventory, 600

Teacher-Pupil Question Inventory—Revised, 1266

Teacher-Pupil Relationship Inventory, 256

Teacher-Pupil Response Inventory, 1267

Teacher Pupil Survey, 5006

Teacher Questionnaire Regarding Moonlighting, 226

Teacher Rating Form, 962, 963

Teacher Rating Questionnaire, 1028

Teacher Rating Scale, 1063, 1570, 2395, 2890, 5391

Teacher Rating Scale of Children's Actual Competence, 3688

Teacher Rating Scales, 3606

Teacher Ratings of Pupils, 298

Teacher Report Form, 6325

Teacher Scoring Keys, 3604

Teacher Sex Role Adoption Ratings, 881

Teacher Stress Inventory, 2666, 4207, 4208

Teacher Stress Inventory—Revised, 4209

Teacher Stress Measure, 4210

Teacher Style Instrument, 333

Teacher Support Behavior Survey, 7341

Teacher Survey, 6178

Teacher Temperament Questionnaire, 1884, 3380

Teacher Temperament Questionnaire—Short Form, 3381

Teacher Tolerance Scale, 5008

Teacher Treatment Inventory, 2892, 6966

Teacher Treatment Inventory, Revised, 4469

Teacher Work Autonomy Scale, 5009

Teachers Attitude Inventory, 559

Teacher's Behavior Rating Scale, 582

Teachers' Beliefs about Administrators, 5007

Teachers' Beliefs about Parents, 4629

Teachers' Elementary Guidance Opinionnaire, 332

Teacher's Evaluation of Student's Creativity, 2942

Teachers' Perceived School Effectiveness Scale, 6613
Teacher's Perceptions Questionnaire, 4467
Teachers Professional Ambition Index, 1363
Teachers Rate Pupils, 297
Teachers' Rating of Depression Scale, 3949
Teacher's Rating Scale, 4468
Teacher's Rating Scale of Child's Competence, 3689
Teacher's Self-Control Rating Scale, 2891, 4466
Teachers' Vertical Ambition Index, 1364
Teaching Anxiety Scale, 4211
Teaching Assessment Blank, 1029
Teaching Autonomy Scale, 6967
Teaching Behavior Scale for Child Tutors, 2893
Teaching Effectiveness Instrument, 3607
Teaching Effectiveness Questionnaire, 3330
Teaching Effectiveness Scale, 1030
Teaching Environment Scale, 6614
Teaching Evaluation Questionnaire, 1569, 7342
Teaching in Urban Schools Questionnaire, 1593
Teaching Requirements for Counselor Certification Questionnaire, 702
Teaching Style Inventory, 882
Teaching Style Questionnaire, 1571
Teaching Younger Siblings Questionnaire, 6326
Team Efficacy Scale, 6615
Team-Member Exchange Scale, 6358
Team Teaching Attitude Questionnaire, 334
Tedium Burnout Scale, 3950
Tedium Measure, 2540
Tedium Scale, 5690

Teenager's Self-Test: Drug Use, 4470
Tel-Aviv Activities Inventory, 6327
Tel Aviv Locus of Control, 2148
Tellegen Absorption Scale, 5214 [See also Absorption Scale]
Templar Death Anxiety Scale, 2541, 5691 [See also Death Anxiety Scale]
Temporal Dimensions Questionnaire, 4683
Temporal Integration Scales, 3335
Temporal Lobe Scale, 5155
Temporal Memory Span I Motion Picture Test, 1436
Temporal Memory Span II Motion Picture Test, 1437
Tendency for Premature Critical Evaluations of Ideas in Problem Solving Scale, 5156
Tendency to Gossip Questionnaire, 7053
Tennessee Self-Concept Scale, 255
Tension Index, 1690, 2542
Tension Scale, 2667
Termination Behavior Checklist, 4471
Termination Behavior Checklist—Therapist, 6328
Test and Class Anxiety Rating Scale, 5440
Test Anxiety Inventory, 1633, 2429, 3742 [See also Inventory of Test Anxiety; Osterhouse Test Anxiety Inventory]
Test Anxiety Questionnaire, 26, 1075, 1634 [See also Mandler-Cowan's Test Anxiety Questionnaire for High School Students—Short Form; Mandler-Sarason Test Anxiety Questionnaire]
Test Anxiety Questionnaire (Short Form), 209, 401
Test Anxiety Scale, 2430, 3743 [See also Mandler-Sarason Test Anxiety Scale; Sarason Test Anxiety Scale]

Test Anxiety Scale for Adolescents, 3744

Test Anxiety Scale for Children, 25, 402, 1076, 1635, 3745, 5441

Test Anxiety Scale—Hebrew Version, 5442

Test Attitude Survey, 2791, 2792, 4333, 6179

Test Behavior Inventory, 1242

Test Comfort Index, 3746

Test of Analogical Reasoning in Children, 7145

Test of Basic Language Competence in English and Spanish (Level I), 380 [See also Tests of Basic Language Competence: Level I]

Test of Conceptions of Justice for Young Children, 381

Test of Counselor Attitudes, 560 [See also Porter Test of Counselor Attitudes]

Test of Critical Thinking, 5157

Test of Fantasy, 1243

Test of Formal Reasoning, 3442

Test of Guilt Reaction, 964

Test of Internal Moral Judgment, 638

Test of Logical Connectives, 123

Test of Logical Reasoning, 5158

Test of Memory Performance, 382

Test of Misconceptions about Psychology, 6968

Test of Number Concepts, 2939

Test of Phonemic Analysis and Blending, 3690

Test of Risk-Taking on Objective Examinations, 1077

Test of Science-Related Attitudes, 2793

Test of Social Inference, 1114, 1619

Test of Syntactic Comprehension, 383

Test of Test-Wiseness—Revised, 3443

Test of Verbal Absurdities, 895

Test on Economic Decision-Making (TED), 2396

Test-Wiseness Instrument, 1064

Test Wiseness Measure, 1620

Test Wiseness Scale, 385, 1621

Testing Practices Questionnaire, 190

Tests of Basic Language Competence: Level I, 384 [See also Test of Basic Language Competence in English and Spanish (Level I)]

Tests of Logical Additions, 19

Tests of Specific Cognitive Abilities for 3-Year-Olds, 2961

Texas Social Behavior Index, 2614

Texas Social Behavior Inventory, 2149, 4103, 5010, 6970, 6971

Texas Social Behavior Inventory— Short Form, 4472

Textbook Appraisal Form, 1983

Theft Scale, 1244

Thematic Apperception Test for Urban Hispanic Children, 3382

Thematic Apperception Test-Type Pictures, 210

Theoretical Orientation to Reading Profile, 6972

Therapeutic Reactance Scale, 4473, 6329

Therapeutic Talent Index, 3383

Therapist Activity Rating Scale, 7343

Therapist and Client Rating Scales, 5303

Therapist Expectancy Inventory, 3336

Therapist Orientation Questionnaire, 96

Therapist Personal Reaction Questionnaire, 4334

Therapist Satisfaction Scale, 4684

Therapist Termination Questionnaire—Adapted, 6330

Therapist's Behavior Scale, 2197

Therapy Goal Checklist, 1365

Therapy Session Report, 191

Thinking Orientation Questionnaire, 7146

Third-Culture Adolescent Question-
naire, 7055
Thought Occurrence Questionnaire,
5692
Threat Index, 1691, 3951
Threatening-Defensiveness Ques-
tionnaire, 299
Three Scales for Measuring Atti-
tudes of Arab Students toward
Americans, 97
Threshold Traits Analogy, 3515
Thumin Conservatism-Liberalism
Scale, 1835
Thumin Test of Mental Dexterity,
2689 [See also Mental Dexterity
Test]
Time Management Behavior Scale,
4474
Time Metaphors Test, 834
Time Structure Questionnaire, 4475
Time Urgency Scale, 5693
Title Recognition Scale, 5392
Title Recognition Test—Form 1,
5393
Title Recognition Test—Form 2,
5394
Toddler Behavior Questionnaire,
3384
Toddler Temperament Scale, 3385
Tolerance for Ambiguity, 965
Tolerance for Ambiguity Scale,
3516, 6973 [See also Ambiguity
Tolerance Scale; AT-20; Intoler-
ance of Ambiguity...; Revised
Scale for Ambiguity Tolerance;
Scale of Tolerance-Intolerance of
Ambiguity]
Tolerance of Bureaucratic Structure
Scale, 1508
Toronto Alexithymia Scale, 7056
Torrance Checklist of Creative
Positives, 1283
Torrance Life Experience Inventory,
861
Total Life Stress Scale, 2543
Touch Avoidance Measure, 5883
Touch OK Scale, 5884

Toughness and Consistency Scale,
5077
Toy Preference Test, 883, 3414,
5115
Traditional Family Ideology, 3047
Traditionality of the Husband
Scale, 6974
Traffic Safety Questionnaire, 1622
Trail Making Test, 1469
Trainee Adjustment Scale, 27
Trainee Equity Index, 6616
Trainee Personal Reaction Scale—
Revised, 6027
Trainer Behavior Scale, 6331
Training Characteristics Scale,
6617
Training Scale, 5395
Training Utility Scale, 4335
Trait Ascription Scale, 5012
Trait Frustration Scale, 3517
Trait Self Knowledge, Rated
Importance and Desirability
Scale, 862
Trait Sport-Confidence Inventory,
5217
Transcendence Index, 40, 41
Transfer Questionnaire, 192
Transition to Parenthood Measure,
3048
Transitive Pantomime Expression
Test, 6359
Transpersonal Orientation to
Learning Scale, 4336
Transportation Concerns Scale,
6028
Trauma Reaction Index, 5694
Traumatic Stress Response, 4104
Treatment Acceptability Question-
naire, 6618, 7344
Treatment Evaluation Inventory,
6619
Treatment of Advancing Minorities
Scales, 7148
Treatment of Animals Scale, 4337
Trent Attribution Profile, 2150,
6975
Triangular Love Scale, 4105

Tridimensional Personality Questionnaire, 7057
Triple Audit Opinion Survey (TAOS), 2668
Trodahl and Powell Dogmatism Scale, 2294 [See also Dogmatism Scale]
Truax-Carkhuff Relationship Questionnaire—Short Form, 1268 [See also Relationship Questionnaire]
Truax Rating Scales, 1438
Trust and Suspicion Scale, 5078
Trust Expectancy Questionnaire, 7259
Trust in Management Scale, 6029
Trust in Supervisor Scale, 2359
Trustworthy Scale, 2151
Tsai Number Joining Test, 478
Tuckman Teacher Feedback Form, 1885
Tuckman Topical Inventory, 1279, 1913
Tuckman's Interpersonal Topical Inventory, 1509
Turner Perceived Occupational Discrimination against Women Scale, 6976
Turnover Intention Index, 6030
Turnover Intention Scale, 6031
Turnover Intentions Measure, 6032
Turnover Intentions Scale, 4212, 6033–6035
Tutor Observation Scale, 322
Tutoring Attitude Questionnaire, 2794
Twenty Statements Test, 988, 1439
Twenty-Two Item Screening Score, 42
Two-Dimensional Sentence Completion Test, 863
Type A Behavior Questionnaire (Finnish), 5218
Type A Behavior Scale, 1886, 3518
Type A Cognitive Questionnaire, 5219
Type A Inventory, 5220
Type A Self-Rating Inventory, 7206

U

U Scale, 835
U-Tube Test, 1623
UCLA Loneliness Scale, 1729, 4108, 5885
UCLA Loneliness Scale, Revised, 2615, 4106, 4107, 5886
UCLA Loneliness Scale—Short Version, 5888
UCLA Loneliness Scale—Version 2, 5889
UCLA Loneliness Scale(s), 5887
Understanding Literacy Behavior Test, 3337
Understanding the Pay System Scale, 6620
Unemployment Attribution Scale, 5013
Unemployment Coping Tactics Scale, 3952
Unemployment Support Scale, 4109
Unethical Behaviors Inventory, 4476
Union Activity Participation Scale, 7431
Union as a Mechanism for Change Scale, 3118
Union Attitude Questionnaire, 1836
Union Attitude Scale, 1837
Union Attitudes Scale, 6186
Union Commitment Scale, 5353, 7432, 7433, 7435 [See also Commitment to the Union Scale]
Union Commitment Scale—Revised, 7434
Union-Family Conflict Scale, 6520
Union Instrumentality Scale, 2669, 6621
Union Membership and Behavior Scale, 2894
Union Organization Questionnaire, 4685

Union Participation Scale, 5354
Union Satisfaction Measure, 7436
Union Satisfaction Scale, 4213, 4214, 7437
Union Satisfaction Scales, 6036
Union Socialization Scale, 4110
Unionism Scale, 3415
Universal Forces Scale, 5014
University Alienation Scale, 465, 1730, 3747, 4111, 5443, 5890
University Climate Scale, 4686
University Counseling and Testing Center Attitudes Survey, 4338
University Counseling Center Use Questionnaire, 703
University Environment Perceptions Scale, 1440
University Experience Questionnaire, 3748
University Homophobia Scale, 5015
[University of] Houston Stress Scale, 2415
University of Illinois Course Evaluation Questionnaire, 335
University of Washington Survey of Student Opinion of Teaching, 1032
University Residence Environment Scales, 704
University Student Census, 705
Unrevealed Differences Questionnaire, 4630
Unsubstantiated Beliefs Scale, 5016
Unusual Meanings Vocabulary Test, 1914
U.S. Defense Policies and Political Protest Questionnaire, 1197
Use of Power Scale, 7207
Usefulness of Mathematics Scale, 6180, 6977

Valence of Job Outcomes—Q-Sort, 1534
Valence of Outcomes Scale, 3416
Valence Scale, 2895
Valence Scales for Mathematics and English, 5246
Value Clarification Questionnaire, 1533
Value Interest Dynamics Instrument, 1535
Value Inventory, 989
Value of Mathematics Scale, 2795
Value Orientation Inventory, 7260
Value Orientation Scale, 7261
Value Scale, 7262
Value Survey, 7263
Values Concerning Disadvantaged Pupils Questionnaire, 990
Values Inventory, 304, 5247
Values Questionnaire, 5248
Values Scale, 5249
Values Sentence Completion Test, 991
Vandalism Scale, 1245
Vanderbilt Negative Indicators Scale (VNIS), 3119
Vanderbilt Psychotherapy Process Scale, 2616, 3953, 4687
Vanderbilt Therapeutic Strategies Scale, 7345
Verbal Analogy Test, 1065
Verbal Checklist, 561, 1198
Verbal Classification Test, 1915
Verbal-Formulas Test, 124
Verbalizer-Visualizer Questionnaire, 1916, 5116, 5159
Verran/Snyder-Halpern (VSH) Sleep Scale, 6332
Vertical Exchange Scale, 2926
Videbeck Need Achievement Scale, 744
Videbeck Need Affiliation, 745
Vietnamese Cultural Identification Scale, 5891
Vindication Motivation Measure, 746

V

Vacation Discrepancy Indices, 5018
Vacation Discrepancy Scale, 5017

Virgilio Teacher Behavior Inventory, 5304
Visual-Analogue Mood Scales, 3954
Visual Analysis Test, 1441
Visual and Auditory Memory Tests, 1066
Visual Arts Achievement Test, 5396
Visual Discrimination Inventory, 1442
Visual Judgment Scale, 1115
Visual Memory Test, 2397, 5397
Visual Perspectives Test, 1443
Visuo-Spatial Memory Test, 2152
Vividness of Imagery Scale, 2153 [See also Betts' Vividness of Imagery Scale]
Vividness of Movement Imagery Questionnaire, 5019
Vividness of Visual Imagery Questionnaire, 2154
Vocational Activity Preference Profile Scale, 5355
Vocational Adjustment Rating Scale for the Retarded, 1033
Vocational Choice Scale, 1594
Vocational Commitment Questionnaire, 3656
Vocational Complexity Instrument, 336
Vocational Decision Making Difficulty Scale, 2233, 3657, 5358, 7438
Vocational Decision Scale, 2234, 3658, 5356, 5357
Vocational Decision Scale—Decidedness and Comfort Dimensions, 3659
Vocational Development Inventory, 1291
Vocational Development Inventory (J. O. Crites), Attitude Scale of, 308
Vocational Exploration and Commitment Scale, 7439
Vocational Exploratory Behavior Inventory, 203

Vocational Information-Seeking Behavior Inventory, 5359
Vocational Maturity Scale, 639
Vocational Orientation of Women Questionnaire, 2198
Vocational Rating Scale, 2155, 6978, 7440
Vocational Role Preference Scale, 3660
Vocational (Spatial) Aptitude Test for Retarded, 479
Voluntariness Measure, 6333
Voluntary Simplicity Scale, 4477
Vroom Index, 836
Vulnerability Scale, 5695, 7058

W

W Scale, 747
Wakefield Self-Assessment Depression Inventory, 1692
Walk a Line Slowly Test, 386
Wallace Self-Concept Scale, 3338
Wallach & Kogan Creativity Measures (Short Form), 619
Wallston Health Locus of Control Scale, 3339 [See also Health Locus of Control Scale]
Walther Work-Relevant Attitudes Inventory, 1199
Ward Atmosphere Scale—Short Form, 3120
Warman's Counseling Appropriateness Checklist, 837, 1336 [See also Counseling Appropriateness Checklist]
Warner's Index of Social Class, 277
Warr Job Satisfaction Questionnaire, 2670
Washington Pre-College Battery, 75
Washington Pre-College (WPC) Testing Program, 480
Washington Psychosocial Seizure Inventory, 4112

Washington Self-Description Questionnaire, 6979

Washington University Sentence Completion Test, 4520 [See also Sentence Completion Test]

Washington University Sentence Completion Test—Form 81, 6384

Washington University Sentence Completion Test—Short Form, 6383 [See also Sentence Completion Test—Shortened Form]

Water Level Test, 1624

Watson Analysis Schedule, 601, 838

Way of Life Scale, 4113, 7208

Ways I Help Others to Cope, 4114

Ways of Coping Checklist, 5696, 5697

Ways of Coping Checklist—Modified, 6037

Ways of Coping Checklist (Revised), 3955, 5698

Ways of Coping Instrument, 3956

Ways of Coping Inventory, 5699

Ways of Coping Questionnaire, 3957

Ways of Coping—Revised, 3958, 5700

Ways-of-Knowing Instrument, 6364

Ways Others Help Me Cope, 4115

Weather Beliefs Inventory, 3121

Webster Developmental Status Scale, 481

Weight Locus of Control Scale, 3340

Weight-Loss Questionnaire, 5701

Well-Being Scale, 2544

Wellness Orientation Scale, 6980

Wells-Bledsoe Motivation Checklist, 3151

Wender Utah Rating Scale, 6334

What about You, 3386

What I Think about Myself, 6981

"What If" Situations Test-III, 4116

"What It's Like to Be Gifted" Questionnaire, 6982

What Kind of Person Are You? Test, 133, 620, 1935

When I Was Born, 2156

When My Child Was Born, 1958

Which-to-Discuss Test, 3152

White Prejudice Scale, 2157

White Racial Identity Attitude Scale, 5892 [See also Racial Identity Attitude Scale; RIAS]

Who Does What, 6521

Widgery-Stackpole Anxiety Test, 966

Widowed Adjustment Scale, 1693

Wiggins Personality Inventory, 3387

Wilderness Purism Scale, 7114

Wile Group Leadership Questionnaire, 2896

Willingness to Engage in Future Interaction Scale, 5893

Willoughby Personality Schedule, 43

Win-at-Any-Cost Sports Competition Scale, 4339

Withall's Socio-Emotional Climate Index—Revised, 583

Withdrawal Behavior Scale, 5444

Withdrawal Cognitions, 4215

Withdrawal Intentions Scale, 6038

Witmer Counselor Activity Profile, 584

Wives' Problem Scale, 1306

Wolowitz Food Preference Inquiry, 3417

Wolpe-Lazarus Assertiveness Inventory, 7209

Women as Managers Scale, 1838, 2796, 4340

Women as Professors Scale, 5020

Women in the Military Scale, 6181

Women's Liberation Questionnaire, 1200

Women's Role Quality Scale, 7115

Women's Social Situations Test, 1731

Women's Work Role Attitude Scale, 4341

Woodmansee-Cook Multifactor Racial Attitude Inventory, 482 [See also Multifactor Racial Attitude Inventory]

Word Analysis Test, 5398

Word Association Study, 706 [See also Yamamoto Word Association Study, Modified]

Word Definition Inventory, 125

Word Fluency Test, 1917

Word Listing Test, 1918

Word Reading Task Measure, 2398

Word Recognition Test, 1919

Work Activity Questionnaire, 7346

Work Addiction Risk Test, 6039

Work Adjustment Rating Form, 337

Work Alienation-Involvement Scale, 2671

Work and Career Experiences Scales, 6042

Work and Family Orientation Questionnaire, 6522

Work and Family Role Conflict Scale, 6523, 6524 [See also Work-Family Conflict Scale]

Work Attitudes Inventory, 6182

Work Beliefs Scale, 5250 [See also Marxist Work Beliefs Scale]

Work Challenge Scale, 5360, 6043

Work Climate Instrument, 4688

Work Climate Structure Scale, 6622

Work Commitment Scale, 7264

Work Demand Scale, 4689

Work Dependence Scale, 1034

Work Environment Perceptions and Job Attitude Scales, 6044

Work Environment Preference Schedule, 967

Work Environment Scales, 4690

Work Ethic Endorsement Scale, 5251

Work Ethic Scale, 5252

Work Expectations Scale, 3122

Work Experience Scales, 4217

Work Experiences Questionnaire, 4691

Work-Family Conflict Scale, 4631, 6525, 6526 [See also Work and Family Role Conflict Scale]

Work-Family Conflict Scales, 6527

Work-Home Conflict Scale, 6528

Work Homemaking Salience Scales, 5361

Work Involvement Attitude Scales, 2797

Work Involvement Scale, 3662

Work Involvement Semantic Differential, 3661

Work Locus of Control Scale, 5021

Work Motivation Scales, 1366

Work-Nonwork Conflict Scale, 3341, 6046

Work Opinion Questionnaire, 3608

Work Orientation Scale, 2676, 3663

Work Performance Measure, 1573

Work Performance Rating Scale, 7349

Work Preference Questionnaire, 2029, 3664

Work Preferences Questionnaire, 5362

Work Preferences Scale, 4743

Work Quality Scale, 7441

Work-Related Depression Scale, 6047

Work Related Emotional Distress Scale, 4219

Work-Related Fear of AIDS Scale, 3959

Work-Related Irritation Scale, 6048

Work-Related Needs Scale, 6049

Work Relations Questionnaire, 193, 1116

Work Requirements Rating Scale, 1246

Work Role Centrality Scale, 2672, 4220

Work-Role Salience Scale, 3665, 4342, 5363, 6050

Work Satisfaction Scale, 2673, 4221

Work Site Smoking Ban Fairness Scale, 6623

Work Situations Questionnaire, 7265

Work Spillover Scale, 4632

Work Stress Inventory, 4222

Work Stress Measure, 6051

Work Support Scale, 4117

Work Tedium Questionnaire, 2674

Work Trainer Rating Scale, 338

Work Values Scale, 4744, 5253, 7266

Work Values Scales, 5254

Workaholism Scale, 6040

Workaholism Scales, 6041

Worker Opinion Survey, 1595, 2675, 4216

Worker Traits Inventory, 339

Working Alliance Inventory, 4491, 6360, 7347

Working Alliance Inventory—Short Version, 7348

Workload Scale, 4218, 6045

World-Minded Attitudes Scale, 1201

World-View Questionnaire, 6183

Worldmindedness Scale, 2798, 5255

Worry and Emotionality Scale, 3749

Worry-Emotionality Scale, 1694 [See also Liebert-Morris Worry-Emotionality Scale]

Worry-Emotionality Scale, Revised, 2523 [See also Liebert-Morris Worry-Emotionality Scale]

Worry Scale, 3960

Writing Apprehension Instrument, 2431

Writing Apprehension Test, 3750

Writing Attitude Scale, 6184

Writing Attitude Scale for Students, 4343

Writing Attitude Survey for Children, 7116

Writing Attitude Survey for Students, 6185

Y

Yale-Brown Obsessive-Compulsive Scale, 7059

Yamamoto Word Association Study, Modified, 871 [See also Word Association Study]

YN-2 Scale, 5079

Youn Scale, 6529

Young Children's Empathy Measure, 5221

Your Style of Learning and Thinking, 2199, 5160, 7147

Your Style of Learning and Thinking—Form C-A, 2690

Youth Correctional Center Questionnaire, 1202

Youth-Parent Conflict Scale, 6530

Youth Suicide Scale, 3961

Z

Zaks-Walters Scale of Aggression, 1510, 2295

Zax Information Profile, 2174

Ziegler Social Deprivation Scale, 466

Zip, 21

Zuckerman and Allison Fear of Success Scale, 2545 [See also Fear of Success Scale]

Zung Depression Inventory, 1089

Zung Self-Rating Depression Scale, 2546, 3962 [See also Self-Rating Depression Scale]

Zygosity Questionnaire, 1292